CW00393540

Günter Wallraff is a West German journalist. Over the years, he has exposed napalm bomb manufacturers, the backers of a right-wing coup in Portugal, torture in the gaols of the Greek junta and the morality of the Springer press in Germany.

In Germany, *Lowest of the Low* has sold over 2,000,000 copies and forced the government to enforce laws regulating the treatment of immigrant workers. The book has been an outstanding bestseller in France and Holland and is being translated into every major European language.

In Swedish, 'Wallraff' is a verb – to investigate.

Günter Wallraff

LOWEST
OF THE LOW

Translated by Martin Chalmers

Introduction by A. Sivanandan

A Methuen Paperback

A Methuen Paperback

LOWEST OF THE LOW

First published in Germany in 1985
Original title *Ganz Unten* by Günter Wallraff
© 1985 by Verlag Kiepenheuer & Witsch Köln
First English Language edition published in Great Britain 1988
by Methuen London
81 Fulham Road, London SW3 6RB
English language translation © Methuen London 1988

Typset by AKM Associates (UK) Limited
Ajmal House, Hayes Road, Southall, London UB2 5NG

Printed in Great Britain by Cox & Wyman Ltd, Reading

British Library Cataloguing in Publication Data

Wallraff, Günter, *1942–*
Lowest of the low
1. West Germany. Migrant personnel.
Social conditions
I. Title
305.5′62

ISBN 0-413-19680-1

This book is sold subject to the condition
that it shall not, by way of trade or otherwise,
be lent, resold, hired out, or otherwise circulated
without the publisher's prior consent in any form
of binding or cover other than that in which it
is published and without a similar condition
including this condition being imposed
on the subsequent purchaser.

CONTENTS

for
Cemal Kemal Altun
Semra Ertan
Selcuk Sevinc
and all the others

ACKNOWLEDGEMENTS

I would like to thank all the friends and colleagues who helped to make this book: Levent (Ali) Sinirlioglu, who lent me his name, Taner Alday, Mathias Altenburg, Frank Berger, Anna Bödeker, Levent Direkoglu, Emine Erdem, Hüseyin Erdem, Sükrü Eren, Paul Esser, Jörg Gfrörer, Uwe Herzog, Bekir Karadeniz, Röza Krug, Gesine Lassen, Klaus Liebe-Harkort, Claudia Marquardt, Hans-Peter Martin, Werner Merz, Heinrich Pachl, Franz Pelster, Frank Reglin, Ilse Rilke, Harry Rosina, Ayetel Sayin, Klaus Schmidt, Hinrich Schulze and Günter Zint. Special thanks are due to Professor Dr Armin Klümper, Freiburg, who 'backed me up' with his medical skill, so that despite a slipped disc I was able to endure the heaviest physical work.

A large part of my earnings from the sale of this book will be placed at the disposal of Ausländersolidarität, a newly-established foundation. The available funds are intended to fund free advice for immigrants, legal aid, information campaigns and a housing project for Germans and immigrants.

Not all the experiences and available evidence could be used in this book. At the moment a number of friends and colleagues are continuing to work on other aspects of the same theme. Anyone who would like to pass on information should get in touch with either:

Hilfsfonds 'Ausländersolidarität'
Post box 301443
5000 Cologne 30
BFG Köln, Acc. no. 1149929200
BLZ 37010111

or
Günter Wallraff
c/o Verlag Kiepenheuer & Witsch
Rondorfer Strasse 5
5000 Cologne 51.

Günter Wallraff
Cologne, 7 October 1985

INTRODUCTION

There is a massive sea-change going on within society as it moves from an industrial to a technological epoch. The immensity of that transition and its implications are still to be understood, by socialism in particular, but its immediate impact has been to render the working class fragmented, divided and weak, while cohering capital for another lease of life.

It is as though we have been set back in a time warp to the beginning of the industrial revolution, when the lives of working people were so degraded and desperate that they had to fight their way up through hard, long, concerted effort and union organization to gain even a modicum of return for their labours and some little human dignity for their selves. Now they have it all to do again, but on a different basis and through different modes of organization. What these are becomes clearer as capitalism's new social project becomes unveiled. But the technology that allows for such a project is also the technology that allows capital to be informed without informing, survey without being surveyed and keep its machinations secret – not least through a media that propagates a culture of indifference and promotes a politics of disinformation.

The Fourth Estate no longer even pretends to reveal the deceits of power or investigate the predicament of the powerless, nor journalists try to take us to the heart of a matter. Wallraff, in terms of tradition, may well be the last of a line, but in the way he immerses himself in his subject while standing outside it – in his own skin – looking at the system that makes such subjects possible, he is the progenitor of a new. For it is only such a mix of drama and documentary, of investigative and campaigning journalism, of turning cases into issues, that can now break through the *cordon sanitaire* of the mass media and speak directly to the public about the matters that concern them (if only they knew). And when those he has exposed take up arms against him and use the whole panoply of power – from threats to his person and law suits, to media and state reprisal – to discredit him or vilify him or in some way still his voice, he gathers to himself a public that now calls into question the institutions of society and the apparatuses of the state. And the crusade is no longer that of one man, but of a nation.

In his previous avatars, Wallraff has variously hired himself as a labourer to a landed aristocrat to expose feudal work relations; infiltrated factory management in the guise of a ministry official to show how industry is developing its own armed units to defend itself against worker militancy; passed himself off as an extreme-right German financier, with arms and aid at his disposal, to uncover Spinola's planned coup to re-establish fascism in Portugal; and re-entered into himself as a journalist to investigate the gutter-press journalism of *Bild-Zeitung* (and its ilk) and show how it manipulates news in order to keep its readership in a state of ignorance and so make them a party to their own defeat. 'It cons its readers so well,' says Wallraff, 'that they take pleasure in being kept down.' And in the course of these journeys into truth, Wallraff uncovers too the complicity of the church and of the state in keeping the powerless powerless.

Here, in his latest journey, his most recent incarnation, Wallraff is Ali, an immigrant Turkish worker, the lowest of the low, the under-class, the lump. And like any Turkish worker (legal or otherwise), he is hired and fired, sat upon and spat upon, used and abused, vilified, reified and thrown on a heap (in

Turkey preferably) when he is done with. And like all foreign
workers the jobs he gets to do are, by and large, dirty, dangerous,
temporary, exhausting, ill-paid and, often, illicit. The least of
these is in the sundry jobs he carries out for small private
employers or even for McDonald's where he turns over endless
hamburgers on a red-hot grill in spitting fat, for a pittance. But it
is when, like most foreign workers, he ends up on building sites
and in factories that he finally understands that he is no more
than a unit of labour in the keeping of a subcontractor, who hires
him out at will to a contractor who has contracted to do the shit
work for reputable firms who want to remain reputable. He
unblocks lavatories on work sites ankle-deep in piss and covered
in racist graffiti; removes 'half-frozen mounds of sludge' from
giant pipes high up on buildings (without protective helmet or
clothing) in 17 degrees of frost; shovels (and inhales) coke dust
hour after hour below ground level; is sent into areas filled with
noxious gases (the supervisor asserting that the test machines
registering dangerous levels 'can't be right'); is made to crawl
into a pig-iron ferry to clear a blockage with pneumatic tools and
no mask. And when one gruelling shift is over he is forced into
another with no time for rest or for sleep.

Ali/Wallraff has a choice, though; his fellows have none.
They are permanently foreign, even if, like Yüksel, they have
lived in Germany for twenty years, or they are permanently
illegal because the only jobs they can get are illicit jobs and the
only way they can remain in work is to remain illicit. All of which
delivers them into the hands of the labour contractors who, in
employing them illegally, without registration or insurance, are
able also to filch their wages, of which, when every employer and
subemployer and sub-subemployer has his cut, there is hardly
anything left. There is only work – hard, endless, back-breaking,
soul-searing work – that clogs up the lungs with dust and
suffuses the system with heavy metal poisoning and, if you are
lucky to find a comparatively light job like cleaning out a nuclear

power station, leaves you with a lingering cancer that might only be discovered long after you have returned 'home'. Or you might hire your body out to the pharmaceutical industry to be experimented on with risky combinations of drugs that would not necessarily advance the cause of science but would certainly provide new and expanded markets for old products under new names.

The unacceptable face of the Turk hides also the unacceptable face of capitalism. The racism that defines him as inferior, fit only for dirty jobs and disposable, and locks him permanently into an under-class, is also that which hides from the public gaze the murkier doings of industry. And contracting out the shit work allows management itself to avert its face from its own seamy activities. That also saves it from the legal consequences of employing unregistered, uninsured workers and/or trans-gressing safety regulations – for these are the responsibility of the firm that hires out the labour. But since that labour is alien, foreign, and therefore rightless, the law does not want to know. Nor does the government, which wants the work – cheap, unorganized, invisible – but not the workers. And all the complicated legislation and regulations regarding foreign workers, since the Gastarbeiter system broke down in the early 1970's,[1] have pointed to a policy which builds repatriation into every aspect of the 'immigrant's' life, from schooling to work and even perhaps to death and burial.

A whole system of exploitation is thus erected on the back of the foreign worker, but racism keeps it from the light of day. It is that same racism, popular and institutional, that keeps the unions too from taking up the cause of foreign workers – and the contribution of the media and of politicians in making it popular keeps them forever foreign.

And the Church yields no succour. It is indifferent to the problems of the most needy in modern society. Ali cannot even be baptized into Catholicism because that would make him less foreign, more legal. If only he were less foreign and more legal in the first place . . . Besides, what binds the Church, like the unions, is structure, ritual, protocol. It could not just pick up any old cause from off the street. Where would it be if it took up Ali's cry, 'I say Christ for the persecuted.' Or, as Wallraff bitterly comments, 'It's enough having to put up with them in our schools, suburbs and railway stations. Our churches, however empty they are, must remain free of Turks, and clean.'

Nor does the constantly changing, *ad hoc* nature of their work permit them to organize on their own behalf. Seldom are the same workers allowed to do the same job or work in the same place for too long, and, even when they do, they are required to speak to each other only in German so that the 'sheriff' knows what they are up to. Some of them, besides, are illegals or asylum seekers and are fearful of being sent back to a fascist dictatorship with which the German state has a special relationship.

Wallraff, in unravelling one thread, unravels the whole fabric of German society; in using deception to uncover deception, makes a case for open government; and in revealing the condition of the meanest worker, reveals the state of the nation.

He does more. He casts light on how the technological revolution has enabled advanced industrial countries like Germany to export less profitable industries to the cheap labour pools of the Third World, whilst importing what Wallraff himself calls a 'disposable, interchangeable' workforce to clean up the excrement of silicon-age capitalism. And that workforce increasingly comes, not from the classic reserve armies of labour once thrown up by colonialism and uneven development, but from the flotsam and jetsam of political refugees thrown up by rampant imperialism. The fascist dictatorships that Western powers set up and maintain in Third World countries in their own cold-war interests are also those that provide the West with the rightless, homeless, peripatetic labour it needs. Turkey is a case in point.

Wallraff himself denies that he has a political axe to grind. He is not a Marxist and he is 'hostile to theory and against ideology'. He is motivated instead by ordinary Christian principles. But there is a politics in stories truthfully told. And the truth in Wallraff's story comes from his wholesale immersion in his character. There are not two of him, except in the laying of the words on the page, Ali and Wallraff, only Ali-Wallraff. The humiliation he suffers as Ali – 'Stop animal experiments, use Turks,' reads a slogan – is the shame he suffers as Wallraff. The hate directed at Ali by his German fellows – 'An SS-pig is better than a Turkish bastard,' – is the pain Wallraff endures as a fellow German. The hostility visited on Ali as a foreigner is the horror that Wallraff feels for an unrepentant Germany: 'There never was a better German than Adolf Hitler.'

Wallraff, like Benjamin's storyteller, 'is the figure in which the righteous man encounters himself.'[2]

A. Sivanandan

---

1. See Stephen Castles, *Here for Good: Western Europe's New Ethnic Minorities*, Pluto Press, London, 1984.
2. Walter Benjamin, *Illuminations*, Fontana/Collins, London, 1973.

1. THE TRANSFORMATION

I've been putting off playing this part for almost ten years. Probably because I knew what it would be like. I was quite simply afraid.

From what friends told me, and from the many publications I had read, I could visualize the life of immigrants in West Germany. I knew that almost half of the young immigrants suffer from mental illness; they can no longer *digest* the countless impositions. They have little chance on the labour market. Having grown up here, there is no real possibility of a return home for them. They are homeless. The limitations on the right to political asylum, the racism, the increasing ghettoization – I knew about it but I had never experienced it.

In March 1983, I placed the following advert in several newspapers:

> **Foreigner, strong, seeks work of any kind, including heavy and dirty jobs, even for little money. Offers to 358 458**

Not much was needed for me to be on the outside, to belong to an ostracized minority, to become one of the *lowest of the low*. A specialist made me two thin, very dark contact lenses that I could wear day and night. 'Now you have the penetrating gaze of a southerner,' he said. The optician was surprised; usually his customers ask for blue eyes.

I knotted a dark hairpiece into my own by now rather sparse
hair. That made me look a few years younger. I could pass for a
man aged between 26 and 30. I got work and jobs which if I'd
given my real age – I'm now 43 – I wouldn't otherwise have
come near. So, while I appeared younger, fresher and stronger,
at the same time I had become an outsider, *down in the shit*. The
'foreigner's German' I used in my new life was so rough and
ready and clumsy that anyone who had ever made the effort to
really listen to a Turk or Greek living here would have noticed
that something wasn't quite right. I simply left out the final
syllables of some words, reversed the order of sentences, or
often, just spoke a slightly broken 'Kölsch' or Cologne dialect.
However, strange as it may seem, no one ever became the least
suspicious of me. These few little changes were enough. My
disguise meant that people told me directly and honestly what
they thought of me. By playing the innocent I became more
cunning, and I was able to experience a life which gave me a new
insight into the narrow-mindedness and coldness of a society
which believes itself to be so clever, confident, perfect and fair. I
was the fool to whom the truth is told.

Of course, I was not really a Turk. But one must disguise
oneself in order to unmask society; one must deceive and
dissimulate in order to find out the truth.

I still don't know *how* an immigrant copes with the daily
humiliations, the hostility and the hate. But I do now know *what*
has to be endured, and how far contempt for a human being can
go in this country. There's a bit of apartheid happening right
here among us – in our *democracy*. The experiences I had
exceeded my worst fears. Today, in the middle of West
Germany, I experienced conditions which are usually only
described in history books about the nineteenth century.

The work was dirty, crushing and drained one's last reserves;
but worse, was the humiliation that I had to bear and the
contempt in which I was held. Yet there was another side to the

experience. In the factories and on the building sites, in contrast to my work on the *Bild* newspaper,* I found solidarity and won friends, friends to whom, for reasons of safety, I could not reveal my identity.

Just before the book was published, I took some of my friends into my confidence. Not one of them reproached me for what I had done. On the contrary. They understood me; all the provocations I had undergone in my role were seen as liberating for them. Nevertheless, in order to protect my friends, I have had to change most of their names.

Günter Wallraff
Cologne, 7 October 1985

---

*In his previous investigation, Wallraff (again using a false identity) worked on the staff of the *Bild* newspaper, a West German newspaper notorious for its right-wing politics and what might be considered to be a disregard for decency and discretion. (Trans.)

2. THE DRESS REHEARSAL

So as to test whether my disguise withstood critical scrutiny and whether my outward appearance was convincing, I visited several pubs which I often go to. No one recognized me. Nevertheless, I still lacked the complete confidence I needed to be able to start my work. I was still frightened of being found out at a crucial moment.

On the evening of 6 March 1983 the new Conservative government was elected, and the CDU* leaders, together with those who were going to reap the rewards of their victory, celebrated in the Konrad Adenauer House in Bonn. I took this as the opportunity for a dress-rehearsal. So as not to arouse suspicion, I provided myself with a piece of old-fashioned lighting equipment, a cast-iron hand-lamp, attached myself to a television team and entered the building. The hall was packed; every last corner floodlit. I stood right in the middle, dressed in my only dark suit, now 15 years old, and aimed my pathetic little lamp at one notable after another. Some officials found it odd; they asked me what my nationality was, presumably in order to make sure that I had nothing to do with a threatened attack by Iranians. A woman in elegant evening dress asked with a disapproving glance, 'What's he doing here?' And an older civil

---

* Christian Democratic Union: the Conservative party in West Germany. (Trans.)

servant said: 'It's really cosmopolitan here. They've even come from the Caucasus to join the party.'

I got on famously with the bigwigs. I introduced myself to Kurt Biedenkopf* as a representative of Türkes, a leading Turkish fascist politician. We chatted, excited by the CDU's electoral victory. Norbert Blum, the Minister of Labour, made a bid for international reconciliation. He spontaneously linked arms with me and sang, swaying in time, as loudly as the rest: 'So ein Tag so wunderschön wie heute' (on a day as beautiful as today).

I came quite close to the platform while Kohl was giving his victory speech. When he had finished praising himself and his supporters and wanted to climb down, I nearly offered him my shoulder to carry him through the hall as victorious champion. However, I didn't want to collapse under this heavyweight chancellor, so I abandoned the plan.

The numerous security men, all trained to see through disguises, had not spotted me. After passing this test, I was less apprehensive of the coming difficulties. I felt more confident and in control, and was no longer afraid of being exposed.

---

* A prominent Liberal Conservative and regional politician. (Trans.)

3. LEARNING TO WALK

I did in fact receive several 'job' offers as a result of my advertisement. Nearly all were dirty jobs at hourly rates of between five and nine marks.* All of these jobs were temporary. I tried a few, testing out my role at the same time.

For example, there was the renovation of a stable in a Cologne suburb. For seven marks an hour, I was given the 'overhead' jobs, that is I had to balance on scaffolding and paint the ceilings. The other workers there were Poles, all illegal immigrants. Communication with them was either impossible or they just didn't want to talk to me. I was ignored and isolated. The employer, a woman who ran an antique shop nearby, also avoided all contact with me as Ali, the Turkish worker. There were only brief commands: 'Do this, do that, make it snappy, stay on your toes'. I had much closer contact with a goat which was running around in the stable, than with the workers; it nibbled at my plastic bag and ate some of my sandwiches.

Of course, the Turk was to blame when one day the shop's burglar alarm was put out of action. And the CID who were finally called in also suspected Ali. Indifference turned into open hostility. After a few weeks I handed in my notice.

My next stop was a farmholding in Lower Saxony, close to the Grohnde nuclear power station. The smallholder and her

---

*At the time of writing, 1985, the exchange rate was about 3.75 marks to the pound sterling. (Trans.)

daughter, refugees from the East, worked the farm themselves, and were looking for a male farmhand. They had employed a Turk once before, so they knew how to talk to me. 'It's all the same to us what you've done. Even if you're supposed to have killed someone, we don't want to know. The main thing is, you do your work. In return you can live and eat with us, and you'll get some pocket money as well.'

I waited in vain for the pocket money. Instead, for ten hours a day, I had to clear nettles and clean drainage ditches blocked with mud. As far as housing was concerned, I was even allowed to choose it myself. The farmer offered me a rusty old car which lay in front of her house, or a dilapidated, stinking stall, which I would have had to share with a cat. I accepted the third choice: a room in an abandoned, half-completed building, whose floor was still covered with debris, and which didn't even have a door that could be locked. In the farmhouse, there were several warm, clean, empty rooms.

Ali was hidden from the neighbours. No one was to have the chance to complain about a 'Turk-farm'. The village was taboo for me; I was not to let myself be seen at the grocer's or in the pub. I was kept like a farm animal – but for the farmer this was clearly an act of Christian charity. Her respect for this 'Mohammedan minority' went so far that she even promised me a couple of chickens. I was supposed to raise them because I wasn't allowed to eat pork. I soon took flight from this Good Samaritan.

I had tried for almost a year to keep my head above water with the most varied jobs. Had I really been Ali, I would hardly have been able to survive. And yet I was ready to accept literally any work. I changed seating around for a Wuppertal restaurant and cinema owner and helped renovate his bars, I shovelled fish-meal in Husum on the North Sea coast, and in Straubing, Bavaria, I tried my luck turning a barrel-organ. For hours, I played for nothing.

It didn't surprise me. Everyday racism is no longer news. On the contrary, it was the occasions when one was not confronted with hostility that were worth noting. Children, in particular, were very nice to the strange barrel-organ man with his notice, 'Turk without work, 11 years in Germany, wants to stay here. Thanks.' – until pulled away by their parents. Then there was the young conjuring couple who were doing their act just opposite me, on the Straubing market square. They also had a barrel-organ with them. They invited me, their competitor, to their circus van. It turned out to be a very nice evening.

Often enough, things turned out less cosily, on a carnival day in Regensburg, for example. No pub needs to have an 'Immigrants Keep Out' sign. If Ali entered a public house, he was ignored. I simply couldn't order anything. So it was quite a surprise for me when in this Regensburg pub, packed with Christian fools, I was accosted with a loud hallo. 'You'll buy us all a round,' called out one of the customers. 'No,' I replied, 'you buy me. I unemployed. I worked for you too, paid contribution for your pension.' The man facing me turned red, puffed himself up (the way Strauss often does) and rushed at me in a mad rage. The landlord wanted to save his furniture and rescued me. At any rate, the unpredictable Bavarian was dragged out of the pub by several other customers. Another customer, who later revealed himself to be a prominent local politician, was meanwhile sitting quietly and apparently soberly at his table. Hardly had things settled down, when he pulled a knife and rammed it into the bar. The 'dirty Turkish pig', he shouted, 'should disappear for good'.

I seldom experienced anger of that kind. But the cold contempt which I faced daily was almost worse. It hurts if in a crowded bus the seat beside you always remains empty.

If integration, although so much discussed, couldn't even be achieved on public transport, I, together with a Turkish friend, thought I'd give it a try in a German pub. We wanted to meet regularly in the same pub, at any time, with our home-made pennant and its bilingual invitation, 'Serefe! Cheers!' We promised the landlords we would drink a lot, but not one of them, and we asked dozens, would have us.

Immigrants aren't usually insulted. At least not to their faces. But behind their backs, people complain about the alleged smell of garlic. In fact, nowadays, German gourmets eat much more garlic than most Turks.

Nevertheless, it does sometimes happen that immigrants are served politely in German pubs. If they're served by immigrants. I had one such experience in Gürzenich, in Cologne, during carnival. It had already surprised me a lot that I, as a Turk, was let in at all. And then, when I was treated in an especially friendly manner by the Yugoslav waiters, I almost felt at ease. However, when the singing and linking of arms began, I sat like a rock amidst the swaying jollity. No one wanted to link arms with me.

From time to time the racism breaks out into the open, most regularly at football internationals. Weeks before the Germany-Turkey game in summer 1983 in the West Berlin Olympic Stadium, Mayor Richard von Weizsäcker,* pleaded on television with the population: We want this Germany-Turkey football game to be a symbol of the good and peaceful relationships between Germans and Turks in our city. We want it to bear witness to understanding between nations.' To this end there was an unprecedented police presence at the match.

I too wanted to have a look at the game and got a ticket for the German section of the stand. Actually, I didn't want to hide my Turkish identity, and even brought a Turkish hat with a crescent moon and a little flag with me. I quickly got rid of both. I found myself in a block of young German neo-Nazis. Well, what does

---

* Now West German president. (Trans.)

neo-Nazi mean? Each one of them as an individual may be a decent person, most have open friendly faces. But in this crowd they were distorted masks. Trembling with fear, I denied, for the first and last time, that I was a Turk, even gave up my clumsy speech and spoke plain German to the fanatic supporters. Nevertheless, they still took me to be an immigrant, threw cigarettes in my hair, poured beer over me. Never before in my life have approaching policemen been so welcome. I had never dreamed that I would ever experience them as a force for order. 'Sieg heil' was roared out, and 'Death to the Red Front!' There was continuous chanting of 'Turks out, out, out of our country' and 'Germany for the Germans!' Fortunately, no blood flowed – there were hardly any more injured than at 'normal' internationals. What might have happened if the German team had lost doesn't bear thinking about. I am anything but a football fan, but there in the Olympic Stadium I cheered on the German team.

4. INTELLIGENCE AS A RAW MATERIAL

Ali went to the Ash Wednesday event at Passau, at which CSU boss, Strauss*, spoke of 7,000 supporters. I don't know if a gipsy at a Nazi meeting in the Munich Bürgerbräukeller would have felt like I did. I think I felt at least something of it – Ali remained the leper from whom people kept their distance.

It is 9 am in Passau. I don't need to go looking for the Nibelungenhalle, where the event is taking place. Strauss fans – among them a high proportion of non-Bavarians – are streaming towards it from all directions. Strauss will begin at 11 am, but two hours before that the benches along the long tables are already almost full. The air in the huge hall is full of smoke, most people here have already drunk several pints of beer. Vast quantities of fish and cheese are being ordered. It is the first day of Lent.

I make for one of the few empty places. Before I can squeeze myself onto the end of the bench, my neighbour at the table spreads himself out. And he greets me with: 'Oh my, what's this now? We don't even get peace from these mule-drivers in here. Don't you know where you belong?'

I'm stared at from all sides. The politically aware citizen on

---

* CSU is the Christian Social Union, the ruling Conservative party in Bavaria, elsewhere in Germany called the Christian Democratic Union. Under its leader, Franz-Josef Strauss, the CSU has been a populist, largely Catholic party. (Trans.)

my left is already so full of beer that it's running out of the corners of his mouth. I try to create a pleasant atmosphere. 'I am great friend of Strauss. Is a strong man.' Roars of laughter in reply. 'Go on, did you hear that? He wants to be a friend of Strauss. That's a good one.' They only leave off when a strapping waitress comes past. Her low-cut regional dress and, above all, the precious beer she carries, are more interesting.

I could have done with a mouthful of beer myself. I don't get anything, I'm ignored. So I go to the bar myself. But my order isn't taken there either. At the third attempt, the barman hisses at me, 'Go on, beat it, but fast.'

Meanwhile, amidst a great deal of noise, Strauss himself has entered the hall to the strains of the Bavarian march. The stewards make way for him through the cheering crowd to the platform, where his wife, Marianne, is waiting. The non-Bavarians are especially enthusiastic, waving their banners ('the Peine Delegation at Passau for the seventh time!') and bawling.

Strauss's speech lasts three hours. It's difficult to follow in the midst of this sweating mass. As it is, its logic probably only really becomes clear after six pints of beer. 'We are a party of intelligent people, we have an intelligent electorate, and that's why we have a majority in Bavaria. If our voters weren't so intelligent, then we wouldn't have a majority.' Thunderous, stamping applause.

The toilets can't cope with the crowd any more. Rivulets of urine trickle down the passageways, and in the hall itself there are even some who relieve themselves down their trouser-legs.

The man up on the platform has a lot to say about the intellect. 'We must make better use of this raw material, intelligence, which, thank God, we have a lot of, despite the waffle of some redistribution experts, who want to level everything down.'

However, first of all, the drunks have to be redistributed. The first aid teams and Red Cross workers have a hard job dragging them out.

There are pamphlets lying on the tables: 'Our Party and Us'. CSU supporters are presented in their own words. A well-fed grocer, for example: 'I've never had any worries about being right-wing. I don't know any party that's better for me than the CSU. It suits me, just as Strauss suits me. I like him because of his build too. He's like me. There's only one thing that can upset me, apart from football, and that's taxes.'

Or perhaps a thirsty Turk in the blue and white Nibe-lungenhalle. I almost have to steal a beer. When the barman's looking the other way, I take one and leave five marks. Strauss drones on. 'In this country we have to pay attention to the ordinary citizen again, to the ordinary man and woman, and not to a few outsiders.' And later, when he's talking about the 'hotch-potch of anonymous masses' and about the 'national identity' that he wants to 'preserve', I know he's not including Ali when he promises 'freedom and dignity for everyone in Germany'.

I want to sit down again, and find two places free. The space beside me remains empty, even when the hall gets unbearably packed. 'He stinks of garlic.' 'You Turkish?'

At last the 'happy Bavarian' (as Strauss calls himself) comes to the end of his Lenten speech. His admirers have held out for five or six hours. On leaving, Strauss is cordoned off from his fans. Even autograph hunters can't be satisfied. At least, not on the spot. Anyone who wants an autograph can throw a slip of paper with the request into one of the baskets being handed round the hall. Nevertheless, Ali finds his way to the Bavarian leader. It's very simple.

I pass myself off as a congress observer and representative of Türkes, boss of the fascist Grey Wolves. This Türkes, a fervent admirer of Hitler, had a secret meeting with Strauss in Munich a few years ago. On that occasion, according to Türkes, the CSU chairman had promised that 'in future, with the appropriate propaganda, a favourable political climate' would be 'created in the Federal Republic for the MHP [a Turkish neo-fascist organization] and the Grey Wolves'.

As Türkes' representative, I'm immediately allowed to see Strauss. He greets me heartily and slaps me on the shoulder, like a powerful godfather welcoming a poor relation from the provinces. He writes a personal dedication for me in the commemorative volume, *Franz-Josef Strauss - A Pictorial Biography*: 'For Ali, with best regards, F.J. Strauss'.

The assembled photographers snap the scene. According to the foreword of this splendid volume, Strauss became a politician 'to perform his instinctively understood duty'. For me, it was my closest meeting with one of the most power-obsessed, anti-democratic politicians of the post-war period, who had already taken me to court on several occasions.

I met Strauss for the first time more than ten years ago, at a platform discussion in the Catholic Academy, Munich (subject: 'Journalist or Agitator'). I sat between him and the SPD politician, Wischnewski. Strauss was in a Sunday mood, and wanted to shine in front of the liberal audience in the Academy; he even tried to be pally with me. 'Well, at last I've got the opportunity to ask you. Are you related to Father Josef Wallraff of the Jesuits?' I didn't want to allow him to use such conversational gambits to conceal his hostility to people like me. 'Yes,' I answered him, 'I am an illegitimate son of his. But please don't tell anyone else.' Strauss remained true to his usual form for the rest of the discussion.

5. 'EATING IS FUN'

**Many of our critics are masters at the game of
blind man's buff. They don't take the effort of
doing proper research, let alone looking behind
the scenes at McDonald's. If you don't look,
you're blind to the truth.**

Part of a full-page McDonald's advertisement
in *Die Zeit*, 10 May 1985.

McDonald's recently began a large-scale offensive against
critics in the consumer associations and the trade unions: 'The
attacks will not stop us from expanding even further and so
offering many unemployed people a steady job with every
possibility of promotion.'

An opportunity for immigrants and political refugees too?
Give it a try, I say to myself. There are already 207 McDonald's
in the country and soon there will be twice as many. I try my luck
in Hamburg, and I'm taken on by one of the biggest branches in
Germany, the one on Gänsemarkt. I don't dare lose my sense of
humour now, since our motto at McDonald's proclaims, 'Eating
is fun'. At least, that's what it says in the leaflet given to new
starters. 'McDonald's is a family restaurant in which the food is
good and economically priced. The customer enjoys the
McDonald's experience in comfortable and spotless surroundings . . . We're glad you've joined us and wish you enjoyment and

success as part of our team.' In such a happy team, I take the precaution of passing myself off as 26. At my real age, 43, I would probably have had nothing to laugh about.

Like the hamburger, I'm packaged by McDonald's: paper hat, thin shirt and trousers, with 'McDonald's' written on everything. The only thing they don't do is put us on the grill. My trousers have no pockets. If I get a tip, the hand with the coins slides along the trouser seams in vain, before I eventually put the pennies where the company wants them: in the till. But this masterpiece of tailoring also stops you carrying a handkerchief, so if you've got a runny nose, it drips onto the hamburgers or hisses on the grill. The manager is soon satisfied with my work and praises my skill in turning the hamburger discs on the grill. 'You're really very good at that. Very quick. Most people make a lot of mistakes at first.' 'Maybe it's because of the sport I do,' I reply. 'What's that?' 'Table tennis.'

The hamburger, a sweaty brownish disc, at least 98 millimetres in diameter and between 125 and 145 grammes in weight, bounces like a plastic chip when it's thrown onto the grill. In its frozen state, it rings like a coin striking glass.

Fried or grilled, it's allowed a 'life expectancy' of ten minutes, but it's usually gone long before that. It soon begins to smell if left to thaw. So it's immediately converted from a frozen to a grilled state before being inserted between the two halves of the rubbery soft bap, together with the usual extras and garnishings, and enclosed in its polystyrene box.

'There is so much elegance in the softly curved silhouette of a hamburger roll. But a special sensitivity is required in order to recognize it,' asserts the founder of the company, Ray Kroc.

The Big Mac

'Love is like a Big Mac: the bodies are both flesh in harmonious conjunction. The delicious bun hugs the body in a loving embrace. The

kisses are like a moist shot of tartar sauce. The adoring hearts are hot like onions. The hopes, still children, are green like salad. Cheese and gherkins create a taste for more.'

From McDonald's house journal Quarterao,
Rio de Janeiro, April 1983

The workspace behind the counter is cramped, the floor is greasy and slippery and the grill plate is glowing hot at 180°C. There are no safety provisions. Gloves should really be worn for the work, at least the safety regulations require them. But there are none, and they would only slow the workers down. Consequently, many of the employees who have worked there any length of time have burn wounds or scars. Shortly before I started, an employee had to go into hospital because, in the rush, he had put his hand right on the grill. After the first night's work I've already got blisters because of the drops of fat that spark up from the grill.

In my naive way I believe that, as agreed, my shift will be over at 2.30 am. I get ready to leave and then notice that the others are beginning to make remarks about 'the newcomer' – me. The manager starts yelling at me, demanding to know what on earth I'm playing at, leaving before time. 'But I'm doing exactly what I was told to do,' I reply. He warns me that I have to report to him personally for permission to leave and enquires whether I've really cleared up outside yet. Since I have just been sent out into the cold December night wearing only the thin shirt, I reply that everything is completely clean. However, a particularly conscientious woman worker observes that there's still paper lying around.

By now it's almost three o'clock in the morning. The manager suggests that I haven't got the right attitude, that I haven't got any commitment. It annoys him that my face isn't shining with joy. 'Don't think we're not watching you,' he shouts. 'For instance, you spent five minutes standing on the same spot today without doing anything.' 'No,' I answer, 'not possible, always running backwards and forwards; this job is like sport for me.'

I learn that, in accordance with confidential instructions, night shifts and overtime are only calculated in full hours. That is, up to 30 minutes is rounded down, over 30 minutes is rounded up. But usually times are rounded down. Clocking-in is not done on actual arrival, but on arrival at the workplace. And leaving is the same, first clocking-off, then changing. That way, they steal your time twice.

It is a few weeks before Christmas and the crowds are huge. At peak times, we are turning over record amounts. I earn 7.55 marks an hour, gross, for work that is comparable to that on any factory assembly line. On top of that, I lose one mark an hour food money. After eight hours, the manager magnanimously lets me know that I can pick anything I like from the McDonald's range. When I ask for cutlery, everyone laughs. Cutlery at McDonald's, what a joke.

From my workplace, I can see the customers, and they can see me. There's no chance of going off for a moment to have a quick drink and get out of the dreadful heat. The frying, the garnishes and especially the great quantities of mustard make one very thirsty.

One gherkin to a hamburger, two for a Big Mac, then a slice of cheese and the various squirts of sauce – fish squirts, chicken squirts, Big Mac sauce . . .

There's always too much to do, some bell is always ringing, there's another apple turnover to put on, or a fishburger. And with fingers still smelling of fish, it's on to the next hamburger again.

During the breaks, I try out the food. When I start eating the chicken nuggets, I become suspicious: it could just as well be fish. It has a kind of aftertaste. I get the same impression with the apple turnover; isn't that also a bit like the fish? It takes me a while to work out the cause. The vats are full of hot, boiling fat.

In the evenings, the vats are emptied and the fat from each pan is poured through the same filter, ready to be re-used. Apple turnover fat, fish fat, chicken fat, all go through the same filter. The same filter paper is used for ten pans.

Things get completely hectic when queues build up at the counter at peak times. The servers at the front shout that we're not going fast enough. So I decide it would be a good idea to take out the hamburgers a little earlier. But the manager, he's the only one without a cardboard hat, puts me right: 'You've got no business doing any thinking in here, the machines are here for that! So don't take anything out till it bleeps and don't try to be smarter than the machine.' So that's what I do. But less than five minutes later, the manager returns. 'Why aren't things moving faster?' 'You just say that machine thinks, and now I wait.' 'But the customers, damn it, don't keep them waiting.' 'But who I listen to, you or bleep machine? What I supposed to do? You say and I do.' 'You must wait until the machine bleeps, understand?' I understand.

The magic phrase is service-speed. The so-called 'service aim' is that 'no one at any time should have to queue'. The objective is: 'A minute's waiting time at the counter is too long. This is the very longest anyone should have to queue. Set a goal of 30 seconds. Faster service in your restaurant is a question of attitude. Eliminate 'slow' from your vocabulary. Two per cent of your turnover depends on your response. Long live speed.' Fast food here really is a matter of minutes.

Our branch is well-known for its record turnover. I'm privileged to be present when our boss is presented with a cup by McDonald's district manager. The inscription reads, 'For outstanding achievements in the cause of profit'.

Children have top priority at McDonald's. An internal document from the marketing department of the Munich headquarters declares: 'Fast food is not only a young market. In Germany it is also primarily a young people's market . . . don't believe anyone who tells you the kids don't have any money!'

Layout and fixtures are oriented towards children. Door-handles, tables and chairs are almost all at a child's level. There are special instructions for McDonald's licencees: 'Children multiply your turnover!' There are complete programmes to attract children and, of course, their families. Top of the list is the 'McDonald's Children's Birthday Party'. The fun is tightly programmed:

The 7 stages of a birthday party:

Stage 1	Preparations	approx 15 mins
Stage 2	Welcome	approx 10 mins
Stage 3	Taking orders	approx 5 mins
Stage 4	Collecting orders	approx 10 mins
Stage 5	Eating is fun	approx 15 mins
Stage 6	Games or store tour	approx 10 mins
Stage 7	Goodbyes	

(Internal company memo)

On my third day, after frying, grilling and counter work I start training to work at the tables. I have to clear away packaging and leftovers and wipe the tables clean. We're given two cloths, one for the table surface, the other for the ashtrays. The cloths often get mixed up, because we have to work so quickly. But no one worries about that here; often we have to clean the toilets with the same cloths as well. The food cycle is complete. I feel sick. When I ask for an extra cloth, I'm sharply told to make do with the ones I've got. On one occasion, the manager sent an employee straight from the grill to a blocked toilet. He wanted to carry out the job as quickly and efficiently as possible, so he used the grill scraper which he happened to have in his hand. On this occasion, at least, he received an almighty bollocking from the deputy manager.

Great attention is paid to cleanliness in front of the restaurant. The pavement 50 yards to the right and left of the entrance has to be constantly swept because of all the packaging that is thrown away. So, still wearing only a thin shirt, I am again sent from the heat into the cold.

In the rest room we joke about the cockroaches, which, it seems, are impossible to get rid of. At first they were only in the cellar but now they sometimes turn up in the kitchen as well. Recently, one fell right onto the grill. Once a customer found a fine specimen wrapped up in his Big Mac!

Some of the younger customers, a bit drunk, drop bags with leftover chips in front of me. The greasy potato sticks scatter and are stamped into the floor. Right away I have to mop the floor to get rid of the mess.

A Turkish woman employee has a particularly hard time. As a woman, she's pestered, as a foreigner she's made fun of, and sometimes overflowing ashtrays are tipped on to the floor at her feet. Once someone drops an ashtray in front of me too. As I'm sweeping up the pieces, the next one slams down behind me, and then another and another. I can't see who's doing it. There's laughter in the restaurant. What a joke.

There are reasons why everything tastes the same. This is the verdict of the Consumers' Association in Hamburg on McDonald's products. 'The taste is largely produced by artificial flavours. Drinks contain preservatives to maximize their storage life.' A milk shake contains 22% sugar, which equals 16 cubes or 40–45 grammes. Everything is 'pepped up' to make it more edible. Edmund Brandt, an expert on the US meat industry, reports that ordinary lean shoulder or neck meat can't be used for making the meat patties, because the hamburgers would fall apart. The meat is therefore processed with salt and liquid proteins. 'If the meat is too fresh', then according to Brandt, 'it is too watery for patty production'. If it is too old, it loses colour 'If that is the case, ice cubes are thrown into the mincing machine, reddening the meat again.' And although it appears to be very lean, the finished hamburger still contains 25% fat. Of course, McDonald's customers learn nothing from the company's expensive advertising

campaigns about the wide range of fast food tricks. This industrialized 'as if'
food is skilfully packaged – a kind of Sun for eating.

'Fast food' equals malnutrition and can cause serious health damage.
Nutritional scientists in the US have established that children who frequently
eat in fast food restaurants display increased aggression and suffer from
insomnia and nightmares. This is because the sweet fast food reduces the
Thiamine reserves in the body, resulting in a shortage of vitamin B1, which
affects the nervous system.

As it turns out, I also belong to the company during my
breaks. We're forbidden to go out for a beer or a coffee. A young
woman worker tells me that very often she's not allowed to have
a single break during an eight-hour shift. When she asked about
it, the only reply she got was, 'Keep going! Keep going!'

Someone who wants to see a doctor is told by the manager: 'I
decide when anyone here goes to the doctor.' Once I ask whether
I can take my break yet. I already know the answer: 'I decide
when you take a break.'

There's no works committee here, that is, no union. A circular
from McDonald's German personnel manager contains the
following instructions: 'If you can infer from the conversation
that the applicant is unionized, break off the conversation after a
few more questions, and promise the applicant a decision within
a few days. Do not, of course, employ under any circumstances.'

The founder of the company, Ray Kroc, knows what he
wants: 'I expect money the same way I expect light when I flip
the switch.' And US General Abrams regards McDonald's as
the real school of the nation: 'It's very healthy for a young person
to work for McDonald's. McDonald's makes him an efficient
person. If the hamburger doesn't look right, the guy's out. This
system is a smoothly operating machine, which our army ought
to emulate.'

6. THE BUILDING SITE

It is 6 am at Franklin Street, in the Düsseldorf district of Pempelfort. There are already six unemployed men waiting at the door of the subcontracting company, GBI, when I turn up. Like me, they were summoned here after they had telephoned in reply to a newspaper advert. An employee opens up. The office is on the ground floor: two desks pushed together and a telephone. No documents or correspondence, no shelves, even the desks look as if they've been cleared. There's a sign on the notice board: 'This company registers its employees according to the law.' But no one asks me for my cards, I don't even need to give my name.

Before being driven to our place of work, we have to wait for a while in the adjacent two-room flat. It serves as a waiting room. With its peeling wallpaper and its grubby windows, and without a toilet, it demonstrates what kind of 'status' we have here. A bull-like character called Siggi, who has curly hair, and lots of gold on his hands and around his neck, wants four helpers 'for a nice high-rise in Cologne'. I volunteer and am assigned to the gang.

On the way, in the car, we're informed about the hourly rate and the conditions of work. 'The foreman wants you to work ten hours a day,' Siggi explains to us, 'and for that I'll pay 9 marks – that makes 90 marks a day.'

Half an hour later, we reach the building site on the Hohenstaufen Ring in Cologne. 'Fashionable town houses and attractive maisonette flats with a view of the park under construction,' I read on the sign outside. A ganger, who's already been working for GBI on this site for some time, shows us to the changing cabins. We've just changed when Siggi comes in again. 'I do still need your names for the foreman,' he says. 'Ali,' I say. And that's enough for him.

Our gang is assigned to a foreman from Walter Thosti Boswau (WTB), the sixth largest construction company in West Germany, as I later find out. On the following days we continue to receive our instructions from this foreman and our tools, from the broom to the stripping iron, are also provided by WTB. GBI only supplies workers; it has hardly any equipment and no building sites of its own.

None of us has handed in his cards to GBI. We are all, without exception, working 'black'. We don't even have health insurance. 'What happen, if is accident?' I ask a workmate. 'Then they pretend you've only been here three days and you're simply registered retroactively with the health insurance scheme,' he says. 'They've got a few hundred workers altogether and half, at most, are registered.'

During the breaks, 15 of us sit packed together in a trailer which is perhaps 12 metres square. A carpenter, who was sent here by the Cologne GBI office says, 'I've been in the building trade for 30 years now, but I've never before been on a site where the foreman has told me to report to him before going for a crap!' Some of the men say that, including travel to and from work, they're on their feet for 15 hours a day. 'But you only get paid for the ten hours you work here, there's not a penny extra for the travelling time.'

There is a 50-year-old Turkish worker with us, who is particularly badly treated by our WTB foreman. Although he completes his work at least twice as fast as his German colleagues, he's called a 'Kümmeltürke', a dumb Turk. 'If you can't work faster,' shouts the foreman, 'I'll have them take you away with the rubble next time!'

On Fridays, we usually have to wait a couple of hours after work for our pay. The money has first of all to be brought from some distance away. Some of the contract workers seem to know where these wages are coming from. 'Klose has got to drive to Langenfeld first,' we're told by a German who works permanently, but illegally, for GBI, 'because that's where they have their account, and that's where he picks up the dough for us.' This worker also knows why the wages can't come from a Cologne or a Düsseldorf bank. 'The account in Langenfeld will probably be in the name of some private person who puts the cheques from WTB and other building companies on his account. They couldn't open an account in Düsseldorf, the tax office would be there right away and seize the lot.' We have to wait for two hours after the shift to get our money. Of course, we are not paid for the wait.

It's not only the company bank accounts that remain hidden; everything is conducted secretively in order to conceal our work on the building site. We have to sign a receipt when we're paid, but there's no duplicate copy for us, and we don't get a written wages slip either. After the pay-out, the foreman immediately takes back the sheets on which he has entered our work times. He does that because in the building industry, contract work paid by the hour is forbidden by law. To get round this, 'subs' like GBI make use of sham work contracts, which officially charge the construction companies for something like '40 square metres of concrete', but in fact, they collect the money for 40 hours' contract labour. In many cases the foremen have tables with which to convert the hours of the contract workers into square metres of concrete or cubic metres of earth. In order to prove afterwards that hourly rates were being secretly calculated on our building site, I used a convenient opportunity to distract the foreman and took his sheet. He had written on it 'WTB Construction Ltd, 30 work hours', with dates and his signature.

It has been estimated that 200,000 Turks, Pakistanis, Yugoslavs and Greeks are illegally employed in the building industry alone. That means an annual loss in taxes and social insurance contributions amounting to ten thousand million marks.

The traders in souls often enjoy political protection and avoid punishment. The laws are very weak. Yet the German government hesitates to put a stop to these practices. In the building industry, since 1982, the leasing out of labour has been illegal. Those federal states governed by the Christian Democrats refuse to regard the illegal business as criminal. Therefore the supply of Germans or citizens of EEC countries remains, legally, only subject to a fine.

The police, the investigators from the employment office, and the state attorneys only rarely manage to catch even the small fry in the building business mafia. 'We're barely able to control the problem,' complains the Chief Public Prosecutor of Cologne, Dr Franzheim. More than 4,000 preliminary investigations are currently being carried out in the state of North Rhine Westphalia alone. Contractors have been cheating illegal employees of their wages, or keeping immigrants who are 'unwilling to work' in line with threats and beatings. Cases under investigation – in Düsseldorf, for example – even include extorting protection money from workers and suspected murder.

It's not only private construction companies who, often through a series of intermediary dealers, rely on the subcontractors. The 'subs' also get a share of public contracts. In 1984, there were a number of police raids at the site of the new Düsseldorf State Parliament – several dealers in illegal workers were involved there.

Fifty illegally employed workers were arrested during an inspection at the construction site of the new Munich employment office. And the police are still unaware that contract workers were used in the construction of the extension to the army barracks in Hilden, and for the new Federal Ministry of Posts in Bonn-Bad Godesberg.

Because the Minister of Posts, Christian Schwarz-Schilling, failed to insert the necessary safeguards in the building contract, at least one illegal subcontractor was able to earn a substantial amount. If the authorities had shown any desire to be informed of what was going on, this would have been sufficient to bring the business to an end. The workers were supplied to WTB, which had a considerable share in the construction of the Ministry of Posts, by the Düsseldorf subcontractor, DIMA Ltd. DIMA, in turn, was linked to GBI, the company for which I had been an illegal worker in Cologne.

Ali's first job on the site makes his position clear from the start. Some of the workers' toilets have been blocked for more than a week. They are ankle-deep in piss. 'Take a pail, a scrubbing brush and cloths and sort it out. And get on with it fast.' I sign a receipt for the things at the store. 'It's OK if you sign with three crosses,' says the German trusty in charge, who has a relatively cushy job in his equipment storeroom.

There's a terrible smell in the toilet area. The urinal is also completely blocked. I think this job is victimization. If the cause – blocked pipes – is not cleared professionally, then there will immediately be flooding again. There are plenty of plumbers on the site, but their time is too valuable. Their job is to install the luxury bathrooms of the future owners.

The supervisors and the foremen have their own toilets in a separate cabin. They are locked, the workers are not allowed to use them, and they're cleaned out daily. I mention to the foreman that my work is pointless, and that plumbers should deal with it first. 'It's not your job to ask questions here, but to do what you're told. Leave the thinking to the donkeys, they've got bigger heads,' he replies rudely. Well and good, Ali too has to do what countless other immigrants are forced to do, to say nothing and be glad of having a job. The thought helps me a little, as it does time and time again, to turn my disgust, humiliation, shame and growing anger into a feeling of solidarity with those who share my lot.

The Germans, who make use of the toilets while Ali is wiping up the piss with cloths, sponges and pails, pass their comments. A younger worker says in a friendly way, 'So we've got a cleaning lady at last.' Two middle-aged men chat from one toilet to another. 'What smells worse than piss and shit?' asks one. 'Work,' replies the other. 'Na, a Turk,' booms out from behind the other lavatory door.

Not all of them are like that. There's a German worker who, while he's peeing, asks what Ali's nationality is. When I reply, 'Turkish', he expresses his sympathy. 'Typical. As usual, they tell one of you to get rid of the shit. Any German building worker would refuse.'

Now and then the foreman looks in to inspect what I've done. It's a good thing that he's got a two-way radio, which is constantly bleeping, crackling and chattering, so that I'm usually aware of his impending arrival and can speed up. 'Presto prestissimo, amigo,' he spurs me on, and when I cheerfully point out that I'm not 'Italiano', but 'Turk', he immediately becomes even ruder. 'Then you should have finished the job a long time ago, because you're a specialist in this kind of work, aren't you? Your toilets are always blocked, aren't they?'

One day, the foreman fired some immigrants on the spot, because they had to make an important telephone call during working hours from the telephone box in front of the building site.

During the following days, we drag concrete slabs up to the sixth floor by hand in a temperature of 30°C. We're cheaper than the crane, which has been removed to another site. The following week, Ali is transferred to shifting cement. I have to get the mixed cement across the yard in an enormous wheelbarrow. The barrow tears at the arms, and one has to use all one's strength to stop it from tipping forward. The chargehand, Heinz – also a GBI man – takes particular pleasure in loading Ali's cart right to the top, so as to enjoy watching him just manage to stop it from toppling over. The cart gets heavier and heavier. I put my exhaustion down to the heat. When there's a plank in the way and the cart jumps a little, I can't hold it any more, it overturns and the cement pours out onto the yard. Other workers have to rush over in order to shovel it back into the cart before it hardens. The foreman appears and shouts at me. 'You bloody, stinking animal. Even if you can't count up to three you could at least look where you're going! Do that again, and you can get back to Anatolia and stir the sand with your finger!'

At the next loading, the chargehand leers at me and, despite my protest, fills the cart right to the edge, so that when I start to push, it slops over a little. Oh shit, despite all my efforts, I can't keep the barrow balanced. At the first bend it almost pulls me over and the whole load overturns. There are cheers from some of the German workers. They stand around while I knock myself out shovelling the cement mud into the barrow. I shovel away like mad, looking round in case the foreman is approaching. Fortunately, he's disappeared somewhere inside the building. A German worker points out that the tyre of my barrow is flat. There's a nail sticking into it. That's also why the cart tipped over. I can see the chargehand grinning. When I come past again, he observes triumphantly, 'In time, you're going to work out that you don't belong here.' On another occasion, I catch him in the toilet just as he's scribbling on the wall with a felt-tip pen: 'Death to all Tu . . .' When I try to have it out with him, he spits at my feet and leaves without having completed his artwork.

A few days later, I'm sweeping and shovelling away building debris on the fifth floor when I almost fall into an electrical shaft covered by an inconspicuous layer of polystyrene. I'm lucky; only one leg slips in. Only a slight sprain and a grazed ankle. The shaft is eight metres deep, so I could have broken my neck! Quite by chance, Heinz, the chargehand, comes out of an adjacent room and says, 'You were lucky all right. Just imagine, if you had fallen down the shaft, then there would have been a job going again.'

Another time, a briefcase, with 100 marks in it, is stolen from a

German worker's locker. Of course, suspicion immediately falls on Ali. 'Come on, you were away for quarter of an hour during work, where did you get to?' A German worker adds: 'He should open up his wallet.' Another German, Alfons, also called Alfi, comes to my aid. 'And if he does have 100 marks in it, that doesn't prove anything. Any one of the 15 of us or someone from outside could have stolen it. Why pick on Ali?' It's also Alfi who encourages me to learn better German. He pats me on the shoulder and says: 'Your German's much better than you think, you know. Just try it! You only have to turn the words around, and your German's not so bad at all. Just say "I am a Turk" and not "Turk I am". It's quite easy!'

Alfi was unemployed for several years before the Düsseldorf employment office sent him to the Bastuba company. He stood in cold water all day as a worker on water pollution control and the purification of rivers and lakes, on contracts from the state of North Rhine Westphalia. Only later did he find out that Bastuba hadn't registered him and were employing him illegally, just as they were his colleagues, Yugoslav workers. When he confronted his boss about it, he was thrown out. Some time after that, a friend gave him the address of GBI.

I once asked the Cologne branch manager of GBI, Klose, with other workers present, what the abbreviation GBI stood for. He gave us the following explanation: 'The letters stand for Giraffe, Bear, and Hedgehog, [Igel].' He made fools of us, and most even believed him. There certainly is something funny about our company, and the names change so often that even this story is believable.

We have a new German colleague. Fritz, a blond 20-year-old, has volunteered for the military police, and is itching to be called up. He regards this period of illegal building work as merely a stop-gap. He introduces a twopenny throwing game which we play in the cellars during breaks. The person whose coin is closest to the wall collects all the other coins. I'm lucky and win regularly. Fritz is annoyed and exclaims: 'You Turks are always after our money. You're always just out for yourselves, and you cheat us as soon as we turn our backs.' Another time, he says: 'The Germans are dumb. You're breeding like rabbits at our expense!'

One day, there's a fire in the roof timbers; the roofers had been careless. Several fire engines arrive, with the police. Ali, together with other workers, is sent up to the still-smoking roof to clear up. The soles of my trainers begin to smoulder and burnt beams crack under me. A group of firemen and police is standing beside us, watching as we throw the smouldering bits and pieces to the ground. We run back and forward in front of them, without any protective clothing. We are all illegal workers. They must know, or at least suspect. But they don't say anything. They, too, profit from our labours; we're doing the dangerous dirty work for them.

A German worker, Hinrich, who is 20 years old and married with one child, and is behind with his rent, has been running around for days with a swollen face. He has several abscesses in his mouth and a high temperature. For days he's blackmailed into not going to the dentist. Eventually he asks Klose, the Cologne GBI man, for a health insurance certificate. Hinrich himself hasn't even been aware that he's not registered and is an illegal. He's outraged. 'That's against the law,' he exclaims. 'I'll report it!' Klose replies, 'You can beat it. We don't ever want to see you here again. Anyone who says there's illegal working here gets taken to court for slander. You gave us your cards so late that we couldn't register you. You've committed an offence yourself.' Subdued, Hinrich doesn't dare risk going to the police. The next day he's taken to hospital by ambulance with blood poisoning, his life in danger.

One Friday after work, we are just changing when the WTB foreman appears. 'We've broken the back of it here, now, we don't need you any more.' After six weeks, Ali's time in the building trade is over. A few of the illegals among the GBI regulars are sent by the same company, now operating under the name of DIMA, to another large site in Bonn-Bad Godesberg. The Federal Minister of the Post Office is having a new ministry built. Unfortunately, Ali is not one of those elected to go.

A modern businessman

The 50-year-old Düsseldorf businessman, Alfred Keitel, is among those who in the last few years have accumulated untold wealth. In 1971, he and a partner founded 'Keitel & Frick'; as a subcontractor ('sub' for short), the company rented people to building firms. This has been forbidden since 1982. Shortly before that, Keitel set up The Building Works and Industrial Erections Company' (GBI for short) and continued trading.

When I worked for the GBI in Cologne in 1984, the tax office had long been after Keitel, but his illegal business had continued to flourish. Investigations disclosed that Keitel must have defrauded the tax office of more than 11 million marks in turnover tax and income tax, as well as several million marks in social security contributions. Keitel was committed for trial, and at the end of 1984 he was sentenced to four and a half years' imprisonment. He got off lightly because evidence was produced that he suffered from a 'pathological passion for gambling'. By this was meant his frequent visits to the casino, not the game he played with the 500 people who, according to the tax office, had been earning money for him. Keitel candidly confessed to his business: 'Now obviously I know all there is to know in this line. All the building firms, how things get done . . . only once you've been working with them, you don't implicate them, of course.'

But he still did. 'There are no large building projects without subcontractors. The big companies are all in the ARGEN (Association for Large Building Works) and they all work with subs, all of them. No new building on a large scale is built without subs.'

Keitel about himself: 'If I hadn't been betrayed I'd still be big in the business. No finance office or health insurance office or anybody is going to get a look at what really goes on – except the people that are involved. So when there are trials no one can establish how the individual companies are connected. So you can just work the deal to suit your needs. I can, in practice, pay by the hour instead of a flat wage, but I simply make a different agreement, because payment by the hour is illegal. Who is going to check that? How will the employment office find out? In court you can say, "Prove the contrary!" They can't get at you from the outside at all. Nothing would have happened to me if my partner hadn't lost his nerve. We had tax inquiries and police before. But they didn't get anything.'

Keitel was also prepared to give information about profit margins: *'The worker gets the money in his hand, good money . . . well, not always good money, but the main thing is, he gets it in his hand. Building firms pay between 22 and 33 marks an hour. The subcontractor's share depends on how much he pays his men, how many he registers. Whether he registers all of them or just a couple. Gross wages for skilled men are about 16 marks. Foreigners are always squeezed, they work for bad money, but a German won't. Germans know their rights, just about. But foreigners . . . 10 marks, 8 marks . . . it doesn't matter.'*

A small calculation gives the following results: Keitel makes between 14 and 25 marks for each hour's work. In the building trade, the working day is usually ten hours. Thus, he makes between 140 and 250 marks per worker per day. For 500 workers, that's between 70,000 and 125,000 marks per day. From this income, deduct minimal transport and accounting costs. And taxes and social security payments. Or not, as the case may be.

7. THE BAPTISM

I was a stranger and ye took me in. Verily I say unto you, inasmuch as ye have done it unto one of the least of these my brethren, ye have done it unto me.

St Matthew 25, verse 35.

Ali tries his luck with the Catholic Church. He has heard that Jesus too was expelled from his homeland, that he lived with the foreigners and the persecuted of his own day and as a result was himself subjected to serious accusations and persecution. However, Ali does not come, as one might expect, as a supplicant. He is not asking for shelter or for material aid. It is not his intention to make excessive demands on God's officials or even to lead them into temptation. All he wants is to be baptized!

a) Because he wants to belong to the Church, not out of opportunism but because he has been learning about the life and work of Christ for some time and finds it convincing.

b) He wants to be baptized quickly, since he can only marry his German Catholic girlfriend if he belongs to the Catholic communion – that is what her parents demand.

c) He also hopes to avoid imminent deportation.

(The priests and dignitaries whom he sought out shall remain anonymous. The conversations with Church officials are authentic.)

Ali is recognizably a worker. His clothes are shabby. A thermos flask is protruding from his shoulder-bag.

His first visit is to a parsonage in an affluent neighbourhood; its garden is more like a park. A senior priest, about 60, opens the heavy oak door which is decorated with a wrought iron screen. He looks at Ali with considerable reserve. He says, 'You won't get anything here, go to the social security.' He notices my dismay and before I can state my request, he makes himself quite clear: 'There are so many people who come begging here that, on principle, I don't give anything away. This is a parsonage and not . . .'

I interrupt him, 'I not want money, only baptism.'

The door opens a little further, he looks me up and down with hostile curiosity, and says, 'Oh, I see, we get so many of the work-shy here, who want to sponge off other people . . . Where do you live? How old is the child, and when is the baptism to be?'

I tell him 'my' address, and since it's a smart street in which Ali, by all appearances, would hardly be able to pay the rent for a week, I add, 'I live in cellar there.' And I also add: 'Not a child baptism. I Turk, till now with Mohammed. Want baptism for me. Because Christ better. But must happen quick, because . . .'

He stares at me in astonishment and disbelief, as if I had made an enquiry not about the holy sacrament of baptism but about circumcision.

He pushes the door to again, leaving only a tiny crack open. 'Not so fast, not so fast . . . It's not so simple. There are numerous conditions that have to be fulfilled.' And, with a disparaging glance at my clothes, he continues, 'We don't just accept anyone into our congregation.' When I try to emphasize the urgency of my request by saying that I'm about to be deported at any time, he is not at all impressed. 'Slow down! First, I will have to discuss it with my parish committee. And to begin with you have to bring me a properly registered proof of your address.'

When I dare to reply, 'But Christ.did not have proper home
and shelter!' he seems to regard this as a form of blasphemy for
the door slams shut without further explanation. When I ring
the bell furiously to show how serious my decision to become a
full member of the congregation of the faithful is, he again opens
the door and tells me off. 'This isn't a hostel for political
refugees. If you don't leave us in peace, I'll call the police!' I
attempt to remind him for the last time of his Christian
conscience and his professional duty by kneeling down and
imploring him with clasped hands, 'In name of Christ, baptize
me!' Instead of an answer, the door slams shut again. I really
didn't expect this! Clearly, Ali has come to the wrong address.
There are black sheep everywhere, and in this exclusive villa
suburb, where the very wealthiest want to keep themselves to
themselves, Ali is quite obviously out of place. But he doesn't
give up. He goes to the priest in the neighbouring parish. There,
the villas are not hidden behind high walls, and the gardens
don't stretch out behind the houses; they are more like small
rectangles in front of the door, often hardly bigger than a living
room. The middle classes live here, and there are also blocks of
flats where workers live.

Ali, lacking confidence after his first hostile rejection, asks his
Turkish workmate, Abdullah, to accompany him, not only as a
witness, but also for protection.

It is 5 o'clock in the afternoon. The church is completely
empty. The fully automated bells ring for prayers. But not a
single believer has turned up for the service. Perhaps it's too cold
for them. The church is unheated, and the bitter cold has frozen
the holy water solid in the font. The lonely priest notices us as,
with measured steps, and feeling somewhat ill at ease, we walk
towards the altar.

Probably he was already looking forward to an evening off,
because he tries to back away from us into the sacristy. But I am
too fast for him. 'Please,' I block his path, 'one question only,

want to be baptize and become Christian, am Turk.'

He stares at us, dumbfounded. 'No, it's out of the question. I can't do that. It can't be done!' He speaks in a whisper and doesn't look at us but over us, towards heaven, as if his supreme boss up there could absolve him of his unchristian behaviour.

'Why not?' I want to know.

'It can't be done, it requires instruction lasting several years,' he murmurs.

'But know Christ Book well, read again and again . . .'

'No, I can't do that, I'm not allowed to do it without the cardinal's permission.'

'But cannot every priest give baptism?'

'No, not at all.'

'Not allowed?'

'No, no, no, no. An official baptism would mean admission into the Catholic Church, not . . .'

'Ah, you not really priest?' I provoke him.

He is visibly embarrassed. His vanity has been injured. 'Of course I am,' he answers firmly and slowly.

'Here boss of church?' I insist.

'Yes,' he says decisively.

'Yes, but then can do baptism,' I say obstinately.

'Well, yes, baptism of children,' he admits. 'But to baptize adults I need permission from the Archbishop of Cologne, and that requires instruction for at least . . .' – he hesitates, he seems to have realized that I'm not completely clueless – 'of, at the very least, one year.'

'So long, one year at least . . . ?' My anxious question and my downcast air seem to encourage him in his efforts to get rid of me. He continues, with some satisfaction, 'But it can last even longer. It demands a very gradual, step-by-step approach . . .'

Pointing to the font, I demonstrate my knowledge of the subject.

'Baptize there. Whole body in or only face?' In his eyes, I

must be a complete savage. With a curt 'No', he dismisses my sacrilegious remark.

'But perhaps boss, the archbishop, can put in good word?'

The priest doesn't allow me any illusions. 'I think that's very unlikely! Very unlikely!'

I still don't understand. I want him to explain this rejection. 'So many now want to join Church?'

That doesn't seem to be the case. 'It's not that, not that, but . . .' stammers the priest. The 'but' remains hanging in the frosty coldness of the church: there is no further explanation.

Since he's so utterly lacking in arguments in the transcendental sphere, I tackle him on the practical side. Pointing to the ice in the font I, point out, 'Little antifreeze, and can make sign of the cross.' But this constructive suggestion doesn't move him either. He leaves the church. We stay close to him. I reach the parsonage, which is close to the church, before him, and ring. A small hatch, like at a 24-hour chemist's, opens and an elderly housekeeper looks out When the priest realizes that we can't be got rid of so easily, but that, on the contrary, I am going to demonstrate my fierce determination to receive the sacrament of baptism, he lets us into his office.

'To keep you quiet, I'll look up an address you can go to. But as I said, be under no illusions, it takes time.'

Awkwardly, he settles down behind a huge desk and leafs through a clerical address book. He is in his mid-50s and seems to be healthy and relaxed. Unlike his colleague in the neighbouring parish he is not a bigot, nor does he despise people. He's good-natured really, but lazy. He radiates the complacency of a clerk in a post office which ran out of stamps a long time ago.

I don't want to let him off so easily, especially since he reacts to my request to be baptized as if it were an immoral proposition.

'If I now child, then go quicker?' I ask, cornering him again.

'Yes, if you were a baby in your mother's arms, then, yes. But it wouldn't happen so fast even then. Because first of all the parents must assure us that the child will receive a Catholic education.'

Ali: 'But today many baptize, where parents not even proper Catholics!'

Priest (frowning, uncompromising): 'Yes, but not us. Not here.'

Ali: 'I have colleagues at work, baptized, but are not proper Catholics, laugh because I believe in Christ and talk about Christ's Book. We all have one God.'

Priest (anxious not to be distracted, adopting a completely formal tone): 'In order to baptize adults, I need authorization from the Archbishop of Cologne, Cardinal Höffner.'

Ali: 'And he is good?'

Priest: 'No. I mean, he grants permission if, if, instruction . . . step by step . . . it will take at least a year . . .'

Ali (delighted): 'And he then make baptism?'

Priest (categorically): 'No.'

Ali: 'Have heard that everyone can baptize . . .'

Priest (still unsuccessfully looking for the address): 'Yes, yes, that's all very well, but . . .'

Ali: 'I have also problem: I want to marry, but parents don't let girl be with Mohammed . . . and if I have married girl, then can also stay here, otherwise must go, deport to Turkey.'

My colleague, Abdullah, comes to my aid and forcefully clarifies the problem: 'He must go to prison if they send him back to Turkey.'

The priest ignores this bothersome remark and searches calmly and unconcerned through the address book. He is annoyed. 'Now, where has the FELICITAS address got to?'

Abdullah: 'Because of that he must be baptized very quickly.'

Ali: 'Best if right away, or come tomorrow after work.'

Priest: 'Out of the question, it can't be done!'

Ali: 'Can pay some.'

Priest: 'No, it doesn't cost anything anyway. Baptism doesn't cost anything. Sacraments don't cost any money.'

Ali: 'But if make donation for heathen children, not go quicker then?'

Priest: 'No, that wouldn't make any difference, not in the least.'

Abdullah: 'He doesn't want to do military service.'

Ali: 'I not want to shoot, cannot kill people. Now at home in Turkey a little like in Germany under Hitler. Turkey is dictate . . .'

Priest: 'That has nothing to do with baptism. Those are external factors which don't say anything about the spirit.'

Ali: 'Will be big party then, when baptism is, together with big congregation?'

Priest (as though to relieve me of my illusions): 'No.'

Ali: 'I mean, will be celebration, dancing and . . .?'

Priest: 'No. No, not here . . .'

Ali: 'I know everything, I have read Bible, front, back, back to front . . .'

Priest: 'Everyone thinks that, that they know it all . . .'

Ali: 'Then ask me. Anything!'

Priest: 'Yes, but why?'

Ali: 'Only to see if . . .'

Priest: 'No, it's a question of the regulations according to which adults are accepted into the church. What am I supposed to ask?'

Ali: 'Something about Christ . . .'

Priest (as if I had mentioned something completely irrelevant): 'About Christ?'

Ali: 'About His life or something . . .?'

Priest (as if Christ had never lived): 'Oh, His life? Well, hmm, hmm . . . just wait a moment, yes . . .' Then brusquely, 'How did He found the Church?'

Ali (without hesitation): 'Christ just say to Peter, "You now make the Church for me." '

Priest: 'Hmm, yes, one could say that, yes.'

Ali: 'And now, harder question!'

Priest: 'No, it doesn't get us anywhere, doesn't get us anywhere at all, I'm only raising false hopes.'

Ali: 'Please! One more question!'

Priest (with great reluctance): 'Well . . . yes, why today are there several churches which call themselves Christian?'

Ali: 'Yes, because Luther have other opinion, made revolution, did not believe in Pope any more. So then there are many church which are good. Want to live Christ, but know too little. Want to make own church, because not proper guides, have lost the shepherds . . .'

Priest (astonished): 'Yes, that is quite right.'

Ali: 'I read everything. Also other book with it. The Catesh . . . how is called?'

Priest: 'The Catechism. That is correct. I believe you completely. But that doesn't get us any further at the moment, because to baptize adults I need permission from the archbishop.'

Ali: 'But now if I . . . heart stops to beat and I say, please now baptism?'

Priest: 'In case of death, yes. If there's an actual risk of death . . .'

Ali: 'And if suddenly now have pain then is possible . . . my heart not good.'

Priest: 'Heart isn't good, hmm?'

Ali: 'Always irregular. If heavy work, goes black in front of eyes. Already go to hospital. How called, intensive section . . .'

Priest (corrects): 'Intensive care. But that can't at the moment be a reason for shortening the instruction period. Once you've followed the instruction period, we'll know how far you really are at home in the Christian faith, and if you really belong to it.'

Ali: 'But what good, if must leave. If cannot marry girl, I am sent back to Turkey. And then must perhaps die without baptism, and am not with Christ in heaven.'

Priest (groans): 'Not necessarily. There are certainly exceptions.'

Ali (delighted): 'Then baptize quick after all?'

Priest (a little desperate because of my obtuseness): 'Oh my God! Even if you die unbaptized that doesn't necessarily mean that you are damned for all eternity. Under certain circumstances the unconscious baptism can count. Christ, in his boundless grace, had also given heathens and believers of other faiths, who follow his way, a real chance . . .'

Ali: 'But not certain enough. Better if baptize right away. Come. Now heart not good.'

Priest (rather indifferent): 'Well, no, there are some problems with that.'

Ali: 'But main thing, am then Catholic.'

Priest (desperate): 'Yes, one could say that, but it doesn't count, it's not like getting a certificate. No, and anyway I know you've made this up.'

Ali: 'But is true, can fetch doctor.'

Priest: 'No, it's out of the question, I could even end up being punished.'

Ali: 'But with Mohammed is simple. He first of all say yes to everyone who wants to become Mohammedan.'

Priest (with some scorn): 'Mohammed made it damned easy for you.'

Ali: 'Perhaps more tolerant.'

The priest ignores the reproach and is silent.

Ali: 'But before, when missionary come with invader to foreign country, said: You Catholic, you Catholic, you Catholic! Whether want or not! Why take so long today?'

Priest: 'Yes, but what kind of Catholics! One used to do things, hmm, how shall I put it, very mechanically. Charlemagne said to the Saxons: either baptism or heads off!' (He laughs with relish.)

Ali: 'Just bang, bang.'

Priest: 'That was in 800 AD.'

Ali: 'Indians also had to do baptism, and not know what meant.'

Priest: 'But what was the result! Later they had nothing but terrible hatred for all Christians.'

Ali: 'And then did' (makes 'heads off' gesture) 'to Christians?'

Priest: 'Yes.'

Ali: 'And did the Pope give his blessing?'

Priest: 'Blessing? What blessing? One can cut off heads without any blessing.'

His otherwise benevolent expression gives way to a childlike, inquisitorial grin.

Ali: 'And Pope said was OK . . .?'

Priest: 'I don't know what the Popes' position was in those days, they didn't know what the missionaries were doing over there in America.'

The priest changes the subject and remembers my original request: 'Who wants to deport you from Germany?'

Ali: 'Police, aliens' department here.'

Priest (considerably impressed): 'Aha, the police aliens' department.'

Ali: 'Look, even if I marry German woman, come in bedroom, see if sleep together.'

Priest: 'There are many Turks in our schools here. They were always in my religious instruction class, but they weren't interested . . . they didn't have the least idea of what Catholicism means.'

Ali: 'But now know and want baptism too?'

Priest (aghast): 'No, on the contrary, not one . . .'

Ali: 'Must I learn much, prayers, singing and so?'

Priest: 'You must learn to understand, not learn off by heart but understand in your heart.'

I begin to recite the 'Our Father.' When I come to 'And deliver us from evil', he interrupts and insults me again. 'As a

Mohammedan, you are used to reciting long prayers over and over again, without understanding them. But it's time to stop and shut up shop now,' he says, rising to his feet, determined, this time, to get rid of me. He presses a slip of paper into my hand. 'That's the address of FELICITAS, the faith advice office of the Church; they'll be able to make a decision.'

The director of the Catholic faith advice office, FELICITAS, is a slim, tall, elderly priest. He has the distant, distinguished manner of an aristocrat. He reminds me a little of El Greco's portrait of the Grand Inquisitor.

I don't get the impression that this ecclesiastical institution for baptism-thirsty converts is kept especially busy. I am the only person in the waiting room, and a glance into large empty offices full of imposing antique furniture doesn't lead one to suppose that the bureau has a heavy workload.

Ali feels a little shabby and out of place here, in his worn-out work clothes. After he has insistently and somewhat clumsily presented the special circumstances of his case, he appeals to the priest in charge to make a swift, non-bureaucratic decision in view of its urgency.

Ali: 'Please, so I need baptize very quick.'

Priest (who doesn't take Ali's request seriously, and responds a little sarcastically): 'So! Just how quickly do you mean? In an hour perhaps?'

Ali (delighted): 'Yes, if possible, right away. Many thanks. Otherwise in two weeks at most, because otherwise prison in Turkey. When is baptism?'

Priest (becomes brief and formal): 'I can't say. I'm a specialist.'

Ali: 'Yes, then ask me. I have read all Christ say, and find good.'

Priest (unimpressed): 'Who on earth sent you here?'

Ali (gives him the name of the priest who had looked out the address): 'And he say, cannot do himself, must ask here and get document.'

Priest: 'How long have you been in Germany?'

Ali: 'Ten years. And want stay here. Because I am Kurd, and in Turkey must go to prison. Have done political work against dictatorship.'

Priest: 'Yes, but if you stay in Germany, then you don't need to go to Turkey!'

Ali: 'Must leave, because have no more work, and have permit for only three months. But think Christ better than Mohammed, not so much forbidden. Christ more for persecuted too.'

Priest (who seems to have a different interpretation of Christ): 'Aha, well yes. Apart from your bride do you know any other Christians?'

Ali: 'Yeah, colleagues at work, who also baptized. Only they always laugh when I talk about Christ. Always read *Bild* when I read Bible in break.'

Priest (ignoring this): 'Above all it depends on good relationships with other German Christians. It's not a matter of learning, but of doing! It's a question of living, not learning.'

Ali: 'I happy to do and live. And what must do, so that also join?'

Priest: 'Live with the Church.'

Ali: 'Do?'

Priest: 'Go to church.'

Ali (proud): 'I do. Always go to church on Sunday.' (So that he believes me, I tell him the name of the parish and the church.)

Priest: 'I see.'

Ali: 'And can pray already, too. And sing well.'

Priest: 'How often do you go to church?'

Ali: 'Once every Sunday.'

Priest: 'And for how long during the last two years or so?'

Ali: 'Four months now, always every Sunday.'

Priest (disparagingly): 'Four times four is sixteen.'

Ali: 'But before too, sometimes. But often must work at

weekends. I think service in church very nice. And Christ good friend.'

Priest (who seems to have a more distant, less friendly relationship to his 'lord'): 'But it is difficult to believe in Christ.'

Ali (with the fervour of conviction): 'No!'

Priest (sceptical): 'No?'

Ali: 'He live and show how to live, not just in book, but did Himself, not only say, but live for us. But you ask me now to see if really know . . .'

Priest: 'Yes, well, we can't do it as if we're at school; only through coming together and living and speaking together do we get to know the candidate . . .' (and then, a little accusingly) 'If you had come ten years ago, everything would be OK now.'

Ali: 'And why you not ask questions to see that I know?'

Priest: 'Learning isn't the problem, one can't use artificial fertilizer to make a plant grow faster, everything has its own pace.'

Ali: 'When first Christians come to new country, made baptism very quick, often people not want.'

Priest: 'Yes, well, yes, but at that time the Church had a different strength and a different inspiration. Today the most important thing is to establish what kind of contacts there are, contacts with Christians.'

Ali: 'We not have much contact, because Germans not want to live together with Turks.'

Priest: 'That is the regulation laid down by the bishop. We must all follow the same discipline.'

Ali makes a last desperate attempt to get the priest to act less bureaucratically. 'But cannot I get document quickly? Otherwise aliens' department will take me into custody, and I must go back to Turkey to prison, perhaps torture . . .'

Priest: 'But I can't dole out a baptism under that kind of pressure, because of a political threat! That's irresponsible. No bishop could justify that.'

Ali: 'If I ask bishop myself?'

Priest: 'You won't be able to see the bishop.'

Ali: 'But he live here too.'

Priest: 'But you won't be able to see the bishop.'

Ali: 'But if phone up and ask him?'

Priest (contemptuously): 'Someone like you couldn't get through to him at all. He's not sitting around at home, feeling bored, and waiting for someone like you to phone him up. The bishop is in charge of considerably more than a million Catholics in the diocese. He has a diary as full of engagements as a provincial prime minister. He's roughly on that kind of level.'

Ali: 'But he can baptize, when want?'

Priest (bad-tempered): 'The bishop can baptize at any time.'

Ali: 'And when he go for walk, if I speak to him?'

Priest: 'No, no, that's not possible either. You can't just waylay him like that, he's always surrounded by police.'

Ali: 'But ask one question, to see if I really understand Christ . . .?'

Priest (groans, thinks for a while, asks then): 'Is Jesus God?'

Ali: 'He was God and human, and with it also the Holy Ghost. Three in one person . . .'

Priest (taken aback): 'Ah, that's a good answer, such as it is, the answer is correct.'

Ali (who won't give in): 'And Christ say, He love all people, also those not in Church, Christians should love even enemies, only they don't love Turks . . . I say, Christ for the persecuted. Kurds in our country like early Christians, put in prison because want own culture. And Christ for them too.'

Priest (quite cross, rises stiffly and formally to his feet): 'Well and good, but we must bring this interview to an end now. If you could just make your way back to the first room again. My secretary will show you out . . .'

Unlike the bully of my first visit, this high priest throws me out in a refined, aristocratic way. Here, too, Ali is unwelcome.

Although a complete rarity (there are virtually no Turks in Germany intending to convert to the Catholic faith, and no wonder, given all the hostility and disdain, both open and covert, with which the servants of Christ treat them) under no circumstances is he to be tolerated in the complacent, self-satisfied and self-righteous congregation of the official church. It's enough to have to put up with them in *our* schools, *our* suburbs and *our* railway stations. At least our churches – even if they remain empty – will be clean and free of Turks.

Another priest whom Ali goes to see has dotted his house with rear-view mirrors from lorries. A mirror has been mounted beside each of about a dozen windows, so that any visitor at the front door can first be inspected.

The first time Ali rings, the door isn't opened. He tries again half an hour later, and immediately presses up against the door so that he's in the mirror's blind spot.

The door is opened automatically, and on the first floor Ali finds a middle-aged priest entrenched in his office. He listens to Ali's request without interest or concern, and doesn't ask Ali in. 'That's just an idea you've got,' he scolds. 'Who on earth put it into your head?'

'Christ call me,' I answer him in the manner of religious stories for children. 'I want to follow Him.'

'You just want to put on an act, in order to get a residence permit more easily. Admit it, you are applying for entry to our church for political reasons. You are only interested in your own personal advantage.'

'Christ help political persecuted too,' I reply.

'If you rebel against the law of the state, you will be hunted down everywhere. It's no different here in Germany,' he told me.

'Turkey not democracy, dictatorship,' I object.

'Those are only slogans,' he informs me, 'every nation has the kind of state it deserves. There are nations which are not yet ready for parliamentary democracy.'

He recollects that, anyway, there is an elected parliament in Turkey.

'Installed by military,' I say, 'democratic parties banned and persecuted.'

'But there were reasons for that,' he argues, 'that was the only way open terror and rebellion could be stopped.'

'Police and army make terror and torture political prisoners,' I reply.

'Admit it, you are a communist, and wanted to worm your way in here, so it would be a cover for you. We look after spiritual welfare in the prisons and help every last sinner if he repents. But we have no room for unscrupulous elements . . . it would be best if you go back where you come from!'

I look at him, bewildered.

'Should I have been mistaken in you,' he gives way a little, 'after Easter you can ask me for an appointment again. Then I'll take some time to see if you're genuine, and to test your attitude to Christ more thoroughly.'

Ali acknowledges what he says. But he's had enough. A second interview is pointless. This priest's Christian understanding seems unambiguous enough to him.

'Give my regards to Lord Christ if you see Him,' Ali remarks, on taking his leave, and more to himself says, 'But, no, He's been dead here for a long time.' And leaving the priest standing puzzled, he goes down the stairs whistling his favourite song, 'Great God, we praise thee . . .'

But Ali hasn't given up yet. Surely a priest can be found who takes his Christian duty seriously and doesn't, for the sake of convenient prejudices and barely concealed racism, reject the obvious step of performing a speedy and unbureaucratic baptism.

Yet another two priests ignore the urgency of Ali's situation. A young chaplain dismisses him: 'We do without people who

want to become Catholic to please others or because it suits them. You should realize that we are not an insurance company.'
Another, an elderly priest, who lives in a house like a palace and is a shepherd of souls to the upper classes, lets Ali recite the Lord's Prayer and Hail Mary, and then lets him sing a hymn as well. Ali chooses Christof von Schmid's 'Then went he forth to die in a loving spirit, to win for us salvation . . .', but he is turned down here also.

This priest also manages to put me in a corner when he wants to know what the word for altar-boy is in Turkish. 'Gurul, gurul,' I invent. 'Gurul, gurul,' he repeats, very impressed.

Priest: 'Where do you live, then?'

Ali (mentions an address and adds): 'There in cellar, with Sonne family. No one to know, because not allowed – no window, not dry – to rent cellar at all.'

Priest: 'Are you properly registered at all, then?'

Ali (hesitatingly): 'No, family Sonne don't want. And here nobody rent proper house to Turk.'

Priest (stern): 'Then under no circumstances can I accept you for parish instruction. First of all obtain a proper official registration of your address. And then the preparation will take at least a year. You will see yourself that the instruction will do you a great deal of good. You will really feel at home in the Christian faith and know that you completely belong to it.'

My objection, 'What good, if already in prison in Turkey?' leaves him cold. 'Those are secondary, political reasons, which should not influence our decision.'

Ali wants to give up. He remembers the biblical proverb, 'It is easier for a camel to pass through the eye of a needle, than for a rich man to enter the kingdom of God', and thinks it would apply perfectly to Catholic priests.

Until now, Ali has chosen the parishes at random in the area near where he lives or that he had previously known well. This time he drives out into the country for about 60 miles, and stops

when he comes to the poorest village with the shabbiest church.
He makes for the priest's house. A young man opens the door.

Ali: 'Can I speak with priest?'

'Yes, I am the priest,' says the young man, who is not wearing
the clothes of a priest, but an open-necked shirt. It's the first
time that Ali has seen a Catholic priest without his uniform. The
young man invites him into his office.

Ali begins to describe his problem. Even before he has
finished, the priest interrupts him. 'I fully understand your
situation. And now you would like a baptism?'

Ali: 'Yes.'

Priest: 'Yes, of course. We can do that. In the next few days.
Then you are a Catholic, and I will write out a baptismal
certificate for you. And that will be that!'

Without hesitation, without referring to a bishop, without any
bigoted, hypocritical, pseudo-Christian, inquisitorial questions,
he recognizes the seriousness of the situation, knows what risks
Ali is facing, and behaves with Christian spontaneity.

'Perhaps we should have another discussion together,' he
says, 'and then you will be a member of our congregation and, in
time, we will get to know one another better. And if, in spite of
that, there should still be problems with the police aliens'
department, you can count on me. It'll work out all right in
the end,' he encourages me, 'you'll see, it will all work out all
right.'

I thank him. I notice that the young priest, who doesn't have
the manner of an official, has a slight eastern accent. I later learn
that he had left Poland only four years earlier. Perhaps his own
life has made it easier for him to identify with a persecuted
foreigner, or at least encouraged him to sympathize with me.
Perhaps in his homeland he too experienced what persecution is,
at least he hasn't always lived and worked for a bunch of fat,
complacent officials in the Church. Or perhaps he has only
acquired his ability to sympathize here with us, in the 'free part

of Germany' where he himself may have been treated like an unwanted foreigner.

In any case, I prefer to leave him anonymous too, since I fear that such humane and Christian conduct would be regarded as a serious offence by his superiors and would be punished accordingly.

I will no doubt be accused of having let the Protestant clergy off the hook. The reason is to do with my own real life and is related, among other things, to the fact that as a five-year-old child I had to go through a quite unnecessary baptismal ceremony.

It happened like this. My father was in a Catholic hospital with septicaemia. The doctors thought there was no hope for him and he had been shunted into a tiny room, to die. The nurses, nuns, kept at him all the time, saying that as a baptized Catholic he had sinned badly against his God because he hadn't made a Catholic marriage and had allowed me, his only son, to be baptized a Protestant. In the face of death, he allowed himself to be persuaded that this could all still be made good; another wedding ceremony was carried out, and I was baptized again, this time a Catholic. I still feel the oppressiveness and falseness of the situation even today. A baptismal robe was draped over me, a candle shoved into my hand, and it was explained that from now on I was called Johannes. I protested and said that my name was Günter, but the ritual took place anyway. Even by Catholic religious principles it was a totally unnecessary act, since it is acknowledged that if one is baptized once, then that is valid forever.

Anyway, a few weeks later, my father regained his health. The nuns in the hospital called it a miracle due to the 'active repentance' of my father. They chose to forget that the head of the hospital had persuaded the American military government that my father should be one of the first patients in Cologne to be treated with penicillin.

In any case, that's how I became a Catholic.

This side of Eden

Because they always look so serene and peaceful, like children with their wooden-framed pictures on their red clothes, Ali decides to go and see the Bhagwan boys and girls.

This is a new movement which calls itself a world religion and experiments with new ways of living and working together. Unlike most other religions, here sexuality is not repressed, tabooed or limited to exclusively reproductive purposes. Sex can be light-hearted and playful, free from pressure and not limited to couples. Ali thought that here they would not be prejudiced against him as a foreigner. His friend and workmate, Abdullah, accompanied him.

Unlike Ali, Abdullah from the start had no illusions or false expectations about the Christianity practised by the official Church. But this time, Abdullah had higher hopes and was keen to get himself accepted by the Bhagwans.

Their starting place was the centre in Lütticherstrasse, a good residential area. Here are numerous houses containing the organization 'Rajneesh, Bau Koch & Partner'. The reception room, furnished with light-coloured quality furniture, is all in good taste, nothing stuffy or vulgar such as is often found in 'religious' houses.

As we came in, two sunnyasees were talking on the phones. They were so absorbed in their conversations that they completely ignored us. Apparently, these conversations had nothing to do with missionary work or questions of faith. One was reading through a list of sales figures and kept justifying himself because the sums given were clearly regarded as too low. The other seemed to be giving the person on the end of her phone a quick course in capital investment. She spoke of 'pre-dated gifts' and 'fully legal evasion of death duties'. Then she gave a 'hot tip straight from the US: sell out dollars and get into gold!'

The two sunnyasees look like junior managers or stockbrokers of the informal, laid-back kind, with easy manners (but when it comes down to it, hard as nails). They keep us standing a good ten minutes until one of them is finished with his sales figures. Then he acts as if he has only just noticed we're there: 'What's up?' he greets us.

'Want to be a member,' I say.

He looks us over disparagingly. 'Be a member? But it's not as simple as all that.' And slightly warily: 'Do you want lodging and work?'

'If it's going,' say I, 'But not for money. Don't want to be so lonely. Really live together, right?'

He: 'But that will take time. In your case I think it'll take quite a bit of time.'

Ali: 'How long?'

He (not wanting to be pinned down): 'That varies. We don't have any rule about it. It depends on how much experience someone has had with the Bhagwan and how strong the wish to join is.'

Ali: 'Very, very strong.'

He (suspiciously): 'Why the hurry?'

Ali: 'Want to leave it all behind me. Otherwise got to go to Turkey and prison.'

I tell the story of political persecution. Although he is young and undogmatic and, as he himself believes, on the right way to enlightenment, he reacts just like a priest: 'So am I to understand that you want to enter into a deal because you are hoping to get something out of it, to do with your job or political status? Is that it?'

Ali: 'No. Just want to stay here and belong.'

He: 'Do you want to come to us because you want to stay in this country?'

Ali: 'Yes, that too.'

He: 'That's no reason. In that case we definitely won't take you.'

Ali: 'No. For live together too. Not each make money for himself but in common. And women not one each, but all together.'

He: 'I think it's better for you to stay where you are. It's too far for you to come to us.'

I'd put my foot in it again. At the beginning of the Bhagwan movement, unrestricted common living had been offered, as a bait, so to speak, for all those frustrated souls in the middle and upper classes all over the world. Meanwhile the Master – himself now somewhat handicapped by gout and probably also through fear of Aids – has begun preaching more chastity and living in couples. His new motto is no longer group sex but substitute lust. Luxury consumption for the sake of luxury: Rolls Royces. Aim: a new one every day, 365 per year. Price for each: 300,000 marks. Not for his disciples but, megalomaniacally, for himself alone.

For the little Bhaggies, my demands were too shameless. With certain half-converted gurus of the left, they may still put on a show of living communally, but with a poor Turk come in off the street, the whole structure of prejudices held by the 'master race' reappears.

Another conversation in the Bhagwan Centre in Venloerstrasse near Friesenplatz: there are two women and a young man at reception. The two women whisper and titter when they see the two Turkish candidates come in. When we go up to them, they take no notice and go on leafing through papers. So we have a look round. In a larger room sit or stand about thirty Bhagwan disciples staring spellbound at a television. However, there is no football or Boris Becker match on it. A videocassette of the great Master is on. He's surrounded by an enthusiastic crowd of disciples giving him a standing ovation. He is being chauffered

at walking speed in his Rolls Royce, has rolled down the
window, waves briefly, and graciously smiles at his fans with
fatuous complacency.

Bhagwan's Words

*Selfishness is natural. It's not a question of good and evil. The fittest
survive and the fit must have power. And whoever has power is right. As
Germans you should understand this. I love this man (Hitler). He was mad.
But I am madder. He did not listen to his generals but to his astrologers.
Nevertheless, for five years he was always victorious. He was as moral as
Mahatma Gandhi. By nature, Hitler was a Hindu, much more so than
Gandhi. He was a saint . . . I am completely unassailable. I will attack
everyone and no one will attack me. That is the simple truth.*

From Der Spiegel, *No. 32, 1985.*

The whole spectacle is accompanied by jolly swinging music
and the Cologne sunnyasees rock on their haunches to the same
rhythm as the Oregon disciples; one or two clap in time. Not a
word is spoken.

So as not to disturb their devotions, we go to reception
and I apply again. After we stand for some time, apparently
unnoticed but in fact thoroughly inspected out of the corners of
their eyes, the young man of about 30 turns towards us.
Abdullah has been drumming nervously on the desk with his
fingers.

When I have explained my problem, he replies in an
easygoing anti-authoritarian tone: 'No, that's not the way it
goes. This isn't a society you can join. You'd have to start with
meditation. That takes time and costs 5 marks a dynamic' [he
meant, per hour]. 'When you've done that for long enough, then
you have a talk with the centre co-ordinator about Sunnya's
name.'

The Indian religious leader, Shree Rajneesh, living in the US, has broken his long public silence. In an interview with ABC TV in July 1985 he explained that he is the 'guru of the rich'. The chief aim of his movement is 'enrichment'. 'All other religions take care of the poor,' answered the Bhagwan to the question as to why he did not use his considerable wealth to fight poverty but instead invested in his Rolls Royce fleet. 'Leave me in peace to take care of the rich.' In Germany alone there are at least a dozen discos, a chain of vegetarian restaurants, kiosks and building firms working for the Bhagwan.

Ali: 'What's that?'

He (abrupt and oracular): 'That is what we do here.'

Ali: 'We Turks are often on our own a lot, want to live in common with Germans and others live together.'

He (snubbing): 'You can't judge for yourself what's good for you. Others will do that for you later on. First you must get the feeling for everything else . . .'

Ali: 'But feeling is there . . .'

He: 'You have absolutely no criteria by which you can judge.'

Ali: 'Your boss, the Bhag, is a foreigner too.'

He (crossly): 'Bhagwan is our Master from India.'

Ali: 'So, many Indians too?'

He (reflecting): 'No, we haven't actually. More Germans and Americans.' (There are no Indian Bhagwan disciples. In his own culture, the Bhagwan is regarded as a charlatan. Therefore, India for him is 'a physically and spiritually dead country'.)

Ali: 'Where Bhag live?'

He: 'He is living in America now. People can travel to America to visit him.' (Bhagwan disciples were regularly taken on mass charter flights to the US. 3,000 marks for ten days, disappearing into the Bhagwan's coffers. On top of that, hard field labour for no pay, which is called worship.)

Ali: 'I know that the Germans with you live together in commune. Why you not take any Turks?'

He: 'The point isn't that we live together. The point here is that the Bhagwan is our spiritual Master. Everything else is unimportant. That is the important thing. You can live alone and work outside, and once a year you might go to Oregon, for example. Those who live in the commune must get on and, also, must have proved themselves beforehand.'

Ali: 'We have no work and nowhere to live. And belonging is good. Needs only a little money.'

He: 'That's not the way it goes with us. Having nowhere to live or no money isn't a reason. Just that you simply want to be with the Bhagwan. And that's another reason. You see, we're talking about something quite different. I could say we just don't fit together.'

8. THE BURIAL

Since Ali meets with such resentment from the living, and is being ignored by them, he tries his luck with the dead instead. Why not give it a chance? In order to prepare for the kingdom of the dead, he puts on his dark Sunday suit. To underline his decrepitude, he borrows a wheelchair, and a companion drives him to the biggest and most prestigious undertaker in the city.

Ali arrives without an appointment. He's wheeled in and the owner of the funeral salon greets him politely. At first sight, the woman, in her late 30's, and with a firm manner, is not unlikeable. Ali describes his problem. As a consequence of his employment in the asbestos industry (the Jurid factory) he has lung cancer. The doctor has predicted that he will die in two months. He is here to arrange the sealing of his body in a coffin and its transportation to Turkey.

The following conversation (a little abridged but, otherwise, word for word) documents the macabre, soulless and inhuman death cult of our time, in which someone still alive is disposed of as if no longer human, like a dead object, like a piece of garbage. The undertaker never even once asks me how I am, although I don't look at all as if I am dying. She never asks whether perhaps there is anything that could still be done for me medically. She doesn't want to show any kind of sympathy. Instead she comes quickly to the point.

Undertaker: 'For air transport, it depends on your weight. The coffin has to go into a shipping case and the whole lot is weighed together. The price depends on the weight and where it's going . . .'

Ali: 'Is far away in Turkey, Kashgar Mountain, near Russian border.'

Undertaker: 'Then presumably it depends on whether we go by car, or it's flown out. We have to drive you to the airport, and we have to pick you up at the other end, otherwise you lie around at the airport. And if we drive you the whole way, we can drive you right to the place of burial . . . What is your health insurance category?'

Ali: 'Normal.'

Undertaker: 'Still as a worker, or as a pensioner?'

Ali: 'Sick since one year.'

Undertaker: 'Were you still working until you became ill?'

Ali: 'Yes, in asbestos factory, work with no mask . . .'

Undertaker (interrupts impatiently): 'That's not our problem. The question is, do you want to be driven by car, or do you want to fly? With flying, it's a question of weight.'

Ali: 'I'm not heavy. And doctor say, in two months, when dead, light like child. Because less and less.'

Undertaker: 'Yes, but the length stays the same doesn't it? A child doesn't cost as much, because it has a smaller coffin, and then the coffin again has to go into a shipping case, so that the passengers and the people at the airport are not aware that a corpse is being transported.'

Ali: 'And if not in coffin, but make fire?'

Undertaker: 'Burning. You would be cremated here and the urn can then be forwarded by post.'

Ali: 'That is not so much money?'

Undertaker: 'That is much less, because then, of course, all the transport costs are elimated. If we cremated you here, that would be, everything included, perhaps two and a half thousand marks, and then the dispatch by post – there would be postal charges.'

Ali: 'And can brother not take urn in plastic bag?'*

Undertaker: 'No, under no circumstances whatsoever is that possible, it is not handed out over here. It must go to the place where burial will take place. First of all, there must be an application from the home town, from the place where the urn will be buried; permission must reach the crematorium here saying that the urn will be buried. And only when that document has arrived, only then will it be sent over.'

Ali: 'And not possible, if under table, little money?'

Undertaker: 'No, out of the question. It will not be handed over to private persons here.'

The lady is businesslike and takes the matter in hand herself. She wheels me to the coffins. When I inquire, 'What is nicer, firebox or big coffin?' she responds very quickly despite the linguistic clumsiness, and draws attention to the more expensive transportation coffins. 'You mean urn or coffin? Well, if you ask me, you get a lot more from a coffin. It's quite different. Let me have a look,' she says to my German companion and bends over me in the wheelchair to take my measurements. The heavy swing door to the coffin store creaks, and the cabinet-maker can be heard sawing in a neighbouring room. 'The best thing is, if you take a look round yourself, to see what appeals to you most, tastes differ, of course.' It's almost as though she's saying, 'You can of course try them out, to find out in which one you feel the most comfortable.'

She taps a modest oak coffin. 'This is the standard model. However, if you want something more distinctive and solid . . .

---

* The question is not so far-fetched at all, and has a real topical background, though not in a Turkish milieu. A Cologne manufacturer with subsidiaries abroad, a multimillionaire and strict Catholic, brought his brother, who had recently died abroad, through the customs in a plastic bag. That is, he brought the brother's ashes in a cheap urn, which was packed into a duty-free shop plastic bag.

how would you like this one?' Her voice has taken on a softer, more ingratiating tone, as if she wanted to sell me a marriage bed for life. 'Genuine German oak, heavy, solid. At the moment, this is the heaviest one we have. All solid oak wood,' she emphasizes, 'and entirely lined in silk.'

'Want look,' I say. She seems a little embarrassed; it's as if, in the furniture shop, I had asked to try out a marriage bed. 'Willi, come and help me,' she calls to her business partner or husband in the room next door. Willi quickly comes in. He's trying to look important, but in fact appears somewhat uncomfortable. She introduces me: 'It's about his transport to Turkey. He's only got two months to live, and just wants to look into the coffin.' Together, they heave off the heavy coffin lid.

Inside, there is rough wood. 'But no fine material,' I complain. 'You say, lie nice and soft there.'

The two look at each other like swindlers caught in the act. 'That would still be put in, you can be absolutely sure of that,' says Willi ponderously, 'we fully guarantee that.'

'What cost?'

Willi reads from a price-list: '4,795 marks.' I run my fingers over the wood and tap my knuckles against the oak until it echoes.

'Keep long?' I want to know.

'Yes, that is first-class joinery, that lasts five, six years before it goes to pieces,' he reassures me.

But Ali hasn't yet found the right one. In life he was never given any choice – now in death at least he wants to be able to choose something he likes. 'Is not coffin, that not look like so sad coffin? That is bright and make happy? You know, have always live in dark, wet homes, now at least want beautiful coffin, understand?'

The two quickly exchange glances, but cover up their consternation with a businesslike manner. 'Yes, really bright is somewhat difficult, rather unusual, but what about this one here?' says Willi. The woman wheels me to the pompous, shiny, lacquered mahogany coffins. Each is as hideous and showy as the next; Ali thinks, and says, 'Is that plastic?'

'Guaranteed genuine mahogany,' Willi is quick to reassure me, 'one of our most unusual and valuable models.'

'Little more carve,' demands Ali.

'Hmm . . . yes, you mean wood-carving. Then how do you like our French model here? It's a special offer. It costs 3,600 marks now. Previously it was considerably more than 4,000.'

Ali: 'Come from France?'

Willi: 'Yes, it's from France.'

Ali: 'What you think is nicer?'

Willi: 'It's a matter of taste. This is quite a different type.'

Ali: 'And people who have money – what kind of coffin Germans take?'

Willi: 'Usually the German coffins – the oak and so on.'

Ali: 'And who takes these?'

Willi: 'Often for transporting abroad, to France and also Italy.'

Ali: 'And it keep long?'

Willi: 'Yes – but for Turkey we must also put in a zinc coffin, or a zinc lining . . .'

Ali: 'So, tin . . .'

Willi: 'Yes, but you'll be completely sealed inside, because otherwise we couldn't get you across the border. This is virtually soldered together, and only then is the wooden lid put on top of that.'

Ali: 'How much cost?'

Willi: 'With the zinc inset and the soldering, around 6,000 marks.'

Ali: 'Can get discount perhaps?'

Willi: 'We could talk about the price, if you definitely make a decision and it's paid in advance. We could take 5 per cent, which would bring the price down to 5,700 marks. But only if you actually pay for it.'

Ali (dismayed): 'And if afterwards not die, get money back?'

Willi: 'No, there are no refunds on special discount prices. But you were told, if I have understood correctly,' he comforts me, 'that in your case, it's quite certain . . . that it's only two months . . . until . . .' he stammers. He finds it embarrassing to actually say the word 'death' in my presence. 'Yes, apart from that, we would have to know where in Turkey to deliver the coffin, we would have to add something for transport there.'

Ali: 'We very high there, mountains near Russia, beautiful country, can make holiday with my family, cost nothing.'

He doesn't show any feelings and doesn't take it up. 'I wouldn't go along, in any case. We hire a driver and have to . . .' (he stops and calculates) '. . . yes, we'd have to allow 1.30 marks per kilometre. And for the return journey as well.'

He wants to know where Kashgar is, and calculates 10,000 marks for car transport alone. I ask him, 'If now, while still live, travel there, is cheaper? And then do coffin?' This disconcerts him. 'We are not responsible for that,' he mutters. 'We can only assume responsibility for you with an official death certificate from a doctor, and for cremation a public health department doctor also has to come to examine you first.'

'When is dead, is dead,' I say, 'make no difference.'

I point to a particularly finely-formed piece on display, a graceful urn, simply designed, and not such an ugly pot as the other containers. 'Here, if do fire, cannot go in here?'

'No, for goodness sake, that wouldn't be suitable. That's ceramic. It's only for display. It's not for sale. It's an old piece from long ago.'

I've understood. While my companion wheels me out, I'm assured that the company has contacts in the relevant health insurance office, and that 'discreet enquiries will be made, so that we know how high the death benefit from the insurance would be. Then we'll have more of an idea.'

9. DIRTY WORK

I don't believe it's possible to achieve real changes without somehow being down in the thick of it yourself. I am terribly suspicious of actions coming from the 'outside', which always run the risk of being nothing but empty words.

Odile Simon, *Diary of a Woman Factory Worker*

I'm trying to get a job in a factory in Glinde, near Hamburg, which processes asbestos for brake linings. Turkish friends tell me that it's mainly Turks who are employed on the jobs with the greatest health risks. The strict safety regulations for working with asbestos are not being enforced. The carcinogenic fibrous dust is constantly being raised into the air. Sometimes, face-masks are not even worn. I get to know several former workers. After working there for between six months and two years, they had serious bronchial and lung damage, and are now fighting – so far unsuccessfully – for recognition of this health damage as industrial illness.

The problem is that no one's being taken on at the moment. A few people have nevertheless succeeded in getting a job by bribing the foreman, through 'presents', genuine Turkish carpets or valuable gold coins. Through a dealer, I have already got hold of an appropriate family treasure in the shape of an Ottoman gold coin, when, by chance, my attention is drawn to an opportunity much closer to hand. I learn that the August Thyssen steel mill in Duisburg has for some time been reducing its permanent labour force, using instead workers supplied by subcontractors; these workers are cheaper, more eager, and easier to hire and fire. About 17,000 regular workers have lost their jobs since 1974, and much of their work is now being carried out by workers supplied from subcontractors. In Duisburg alone, Thyssen has 400 such firms under contract. I get to know a 27-year-old Turkish worker who had been sent to Adler, one of the subcontractors, by the employment office. Adler, I learn, sells workers to the Remmert company. Remmert, in turn, hires them out to Thyssen. He tells me about working conditions and methods of exploitation, which, if only reported and not experienced and verified, would never be believed and would probably be thought to date from the darkest period of early capitalism. Well, why go so far afield, when there's worse right under one's nose?

I get up at 3 am to be at the Remmert company's yard, at the Oberhausen-Buschhausen motorway exit, at 5 am. Remmert is an expanding company. 'Services', it says on the trendy green sign. Remmert deals in dirt of every kind.

Fine and coarse dust, poisonous sludge and waste, stinking and putrefying oils, grease and filter-cleaning at Thyssen, Mannesmann, MAN and anywhere else. Remmert's vehicles alone are worth 7 million marks. Adler is integrated into Remmert, like the doll inside the doll. Adler sells us to Remmert, and Remmert in turn leases us to Thyssen. The major part of the sum Thyssen pays (between 35 and 80 marks per manhour depending on the job, dust, dirt and danger allowances), is shared by the business partners. Adler pays a pittance of between 5 and 10 marks to the worker.

At Thyssen, the Remmert or Adler workers are also frequently employed in the production process itself. In such cases, in the coke works, for example, Remmert or Adler workers are working together with, or next to, permanent Thyssen workers. In addition, Remmert supplies over 600 cleaning women to large industrial companies in various cities in West Germany.

A ganger stands beside a dilapidated minibus, checking off names from a list. 'New?' he asks curtly.

'Yes,' I reply.

'Worked here before?'

I'm not sure whether the reply could help or hinder my chances of being taken on, so, to be on the safe side, I shrug my shoulders. 'You no understand?' he enquires.

'New,' I repeat the catchword.

'You go to others in bus,' he says, and points to the minibus.

That was it. That's how easy it is to be employed in one of the most modern steel mills in Europe. No documents, no one even asks for my name; at first, even my nationality doesn't seem of any interest to anyone. It suits me.

Nine immigrants and two Germans are squashed together in the vehicle. The two Germans have made themselves comfortable on the only secured seat. Their foreign workmates sit on the cold oil-smeared floor. I join them, and they move closer together. A man of about twenty asks whether I'm a countryman. I answer in German, 'Turkish citizen'. However, I add that I had grown up in Greece, in Piraeus, with my Greek mother. 'My father was Turk, left my mother alone with me, when I was one year.'

So I need have next to no knowledge of Turkish. It sounds plausible, and the story holds up for the whole six months that I work at Thyssen. If I'm asked about the place in which I spent my childhood, I can say a few things about Piraeus. (I was imprisoned there for two and a half months, in 1974, during the fascist military dictatorship). Only once am I at a loss, when Turkish workmates insist on hearing the sound of the Greek language. Here I am saved by a youthful error, since in my schooldays, I had decided to take Ancient Greek instead of

French. Even today I can recite parts of the Odyssey, '*Ándra moi eñepe moúsa* . . .' No one notices, although Ancient Greek is further removed from modern Greek than Old High German is from the German of our time.

Packed full, rattling and lurching, the bus sets off. One seat has been torn loose from its fittings, and when the bus goes round bends, it frequently swings against the men sitting on the floor. Those at the front then fall onto the others at the back. The heater doesn't work; the back door won't shut, it's tied with wire. If someone was thrown against the door, it could easily give way and the person would fall onto the road. We are cold and shaken when the first part of our trip ends, after 15 minutes, behind Gate 20 at Thyssen. A chargehand makes out a clocking-on card for me, and a Thyssen security man a day pass. He takes offence at my name. 'That's not a name, it's an illness. Nobody can spell that.' I have to spell it out for him several times, S-I-N-I-R-L-I-O-G-L-U. But he still gets it wrong, writes 'Sinnlokus' and puts it down as the first name. My middle name, Levent, serves as the surname. 'How can anyone have a name like that!' He can't shut up about it, even though his own Polish name, Symanowski, or something like that, would probably present problems for a Turk. In fact, the Polish labourers who were brought into the Ruhr in the last century were at first ostracized and ghettoized as the Turks are today.

When I can't stamp my card properly, a German worker comments, 'At home in Africa you probably get stamped on the head!'

My Turkish workmate, Mehmet, helps me and shows me how to insert the card properly. I sense how the other foreign workers there also see themselves as the target of the German's insult. I can read it from their humiliated, resigned expressions. No one dares to answer back. I witness again and again how they appear to ignore the most serious insults. It's probably also to avoid being provoked into a fight. Experience shows that foreigners usually end up as the guilty party and lose their jobs. So, they prefer to stomach the daily injustices, in order not to provide any excuse.

We're rattled through the factory town again, and unloaded at a container yard. Every morning we're left standing here in freezing cold, rain or snow, until the 'sheriff' appears in his Mercedes. He's a strong, bull-like overseer, who doesn't lift a finger himself and whose only work is to divide 'his people' into groups, supervise them and keep the pressure up. Zentel, in his early 30's, a full-time Remmert employee, is invited to Adler's parties now and again and is said to to be his informant and confidant. It's now just after 6 o'clock. More men climb out of other Remmert vans. Frozen stiff, we shiver in the darkness of a container. It's a store for tools, wheelbarrows, shovels, pickaxes, compressed air equipment and suction pipes. There are no seats.

All around us there is a puffing, groaning and hissing noise, and a rhythmical roaring from the factory sheds. It's impossible to see the sky clearly; we can only see the reddish, flickering clouds. Bluish flames shoot from high chimneys. This is a factory town, of smoke and soot, of more than 12 miles long, and up to 5 miles wide, which penetrates deep into the surrounding residential areas.

Things start happening. The sheriff, looking like a mercenary in his khaki-coloured clothes, has wound down the window of his Mercedes and calls out the names on the list. He divides up the work groups differently every day. Different people are thrown together each time. As a result, no regular group which can trust each other is allowed to form. Constantly feeling one's way with new workmates means facing new frictions and rivalries. Perhaps it's just arbitrary or thoughtless, but it may be intentional. In a group in which no one really knows anyone else, solidarity is hardly possible; competition, distrust and fear dominate.

My name is called out. Someone pulls me violently by the ear from behind. It's the chargehand, who wants to make clear to me which group I'm to join. He grins at me; he probably doesn't even mean any offence. We're treated like domestic animals or beasts of burden.

We're set down beside a metal frame tower at the end of a conveyor system, and we scramble up several storeys in the semi-darkness with our spades, picks, wheelbarrows and pneumatic drills. Our job is to knock loose the earth which has overflowed from the conveyor belts and been compressed into massive clods underneath them. We set ourselves a murderous pace in order to warm ourselves up a little. After an hour, our chargehand disappears. Because his labours were more symbolic than real, he got frozen through all the more quickly. We try to get a fire going. That's easier said than done, even though fires are flaring all around us in the plant; molten liquid pours into giant wagons which look as if they're carrying giant bombs, or runs in glowing streams into waiting channels.

The glittering, molten liquid bubbles in vats the height of a house; but for us to start a little fire demands effort and imagination. We look for lumps of coke between the conveyor belts, and break up a few planks which other workers had used for sitting on during breaks. But then we're brought to a halt by lack of paper. Eventually, we do find a couple of empty cigarette boxes and some used Kleenex, and very slowly with the help of a compressed air tube, we get a low fire going in a wheelbarrow. However, before the fire can warm us, we're ordered down again. The ganger appears and orders, 'Everyone down, take your tools, come on, fast.' We try to save the fire, but it's not possible; the wheelbarrow is glowing hot. I can now sympathize with the problems of stone-age people who guarded fire like the most precious, holy treasure. We crawl back into the old van, squat there huddled against each other, and are again shaken through the darkness, which is illuminated by occasional colourless flashes. We're unloaded at Schwelgern, near the coke mill. It's another part of the town, but still inside the factory perimeter. We go down several flights of stairs, below ground level. Only a little daylight filters down, and it gets darker and dustier. The dust is already so thick that I can hardly stand it any more. But this is only the beginning. A pneumatic blaster is shoved into your hands, and with it you have to shift the thick layers of dust on the machines. In a second, there's such a concentration of dust in the air that you can't see your hand in front of your face any more. You don't just breathe the dust in, you swallow it and eat it. It chokes you. Every intake of breath is painful. Sometimes you try to hold your breath, but there's no escaping, because you have to do the work. The chargehand stands at the top of the stairs, where a little fresh air comes in, looking as if he's in charge of a punishment squad. He says, 'Hurry, hurry! Then you'll be finished in two or three hours and get into the fresh air again.'

Three hours. That means breathing in more than three thousand times. That means pumping the lungs full of coke dust. There's also a smell of coke gas, so I feel dizzy. When I ask for an oxygen mask, Mehmet puts me right, 'We don't get any, because then not work so fast, and boss says no money for that.' Even the men who have been contract workers for some time look frightened. Helmut, a German who's barely 30, but looks nearly 50, remembers, 'Six men were killed a year ago by a sudden gas leak near the blast furnaces. They panicked, and instead of climbing down, they climbed up, but the gas rose with them. A good mate of mine who was in the same gang only escaped because he had been boozing the night before, and was still so drunk in the morning that he slept in.'

While we're shovelling the dust up from the floor into plastic sacks, Thyssen engineers who have been working a few yards underneath us come running past and up the stairs into the open. One of them shouts at us, 'You're crazy, you can't work in muck like that!' And half an hour later we're honoured by a visit from a Thyssen safety officer. Holding his nose, he informs us, 'Your colleagues have complained that they cannot work with all the muck you're making. See that you finish as quickly as possible.' With that, he's gone again. The job lasts till the end of the shift. In the final hour we have to carry the heavy sacks of dust up the iron stairs and throw them into a container outside. Despite the effort, it feels like a deliverance to be able to gasp some fresh air for a moment.

During a 20-minute break we sit on the iron stairs, where there's a little less dust. My Turkish mates insist that I share their sandwiches – I have not brought any. Nedim, the oldest, pours me out some tea from his thermos. They share what they've got, and treat one another in a more friendly and gentle way than the German workers do. It's noticeable that during breaks, the Turks usually sit apart from the German workers and rarely speak in Turkish. They usually converse in bad German or are silent, while the German workers do all the talking. On a later occasion, Nedim explains this to me: 'The Germans think we say bad things about them. A few say we grow too strong if we speak Turkish together. They want to hear everything, so that they can keep on bossing us about.' And so the Turkish workers swallow their pride and comply, in order to avoid 'provoking'. I'm present myself on one occasion, when Alfred, a German who's always got a lot to say, furiously interrupts a conversation amongst Turks. 'Speak in German if you've got something to say. In Germany people still speak decent German. You can speak your shitty language in your own shitty country when you get back there, and I hope that's soon.'

The next day we're working more than 30 feet up, in the open, in – 17 degrees of frost. There are warning signs everywhere. *No access for unauthorized persons! Warning. Gas Hazard!* And at several points, *Breathing apparatus must be worn!*

No one's said anything to us about the risks, and anyway, there is no 'protective apparatus' for us. And we don't know ourselves whether we're 'authorized' or 'unauthorized'.

Working on metal scaffolding, our gang has to hack loose and shovel away half-frozen mounds of sludge which have oozed out of giant pipes. There's an icy wind, our ears are freezing, and our fingers are numb with cold. No Thyssen employee has to work outside in these conditions, and there's extra 'bad weather' money for the whole building industry, but we've got to keep at it. First of all, we chip away the outer crust with heavy pick-axes; small pieces of it constantly hit us in the face. We should have protective glasses, but no one dares to make another request. The sludge gives off clouds of acrid smoke, which momentarily blind us. We push wheelbarrow – loads of the stuff to chutes. Our shovels are constantly bending under the weight and even the wheelbarrows have to be beaten straight again. A noise roars out of the surrounding machine halls; it is hardly possible to make oneself heard. This time we don't need the ganger, who's pissed off to a canteen somewhere. We force ourselves to make record efforts, because the cold makes even the shortest pause unbearable. Now and again one of us slips away and runs into a small machine room. Inside, the noise is like being underneath Niagara Falls, but at least the machines are warm. We press ourselves against the machines and literally embrace them, in order to get some warmth. It's a little bit risky, because there's an unguarded rotating rod on the machine. You have to take care not to get a finger torn off. When I hold on to the wrong piece of metal, there's a horrible banging and screeching, and clouds of sparks fly, as if everything's going to blow up the next moment.

Then, still blue and shivering, it's back to the slavery outside. Yusuf, a Tunisian worker, sums it up. 'Cold hell here,' he says. He adds, 'They took more care of slaves. They were still worth something. With us, no one cares how quick used up. Enough others out there waiting to get work.'

Occasionally, a Thyssen safety engineer appears and fiddles around with a box attached to the pipes. He bangs it, mumbles,

'Can't be right,' and looks apprehensively over at us.

I speak to him, 'What is funny box? What is inside?' 'I measure gas with it,' he explains. Then he asks, 'Don't you have any measuring equipment? Then you shouldn't really be working here.' He explains that when the needle indicates a certain level, there's a serious safety risk, and we should leave the area immediately, since otherwise we could lose consciousness very quickly. But the needle has been just past this level for the whole time. When I draw his attention to this, he reassures me. 'That really can't be right. The instrument is defective. I'll get another one.' He brings another one. It takes half an hour for him to return, but on the new equipment, the needle again goes beyond the danger level. Annoyed, he bangs on the box and shouts, 'That's impossible. The fucking thing's still not right.' When I look at him in disbelief, he continues, 'Even if it is right, this level is still no reason to panic. In any case, the wind would blow the gas away.' And he disappears with his magic box again; we console ourselves with the idea that, should there ever be a gas leak the icy wind will disperse it.

Helveli Raci, a Turkish worker, has a similar experience at the same place a couple of weeks later. He tells me, 'There was this instrument which suddenly began to make a hooting noise. I asked what the sounds meant. And they replied that if gas is escaping, then the instruments set the hooter going. And so I said, "There's gas here, the instrument's giving a warning, should we stop? The foreman said, "Not at all, keep going". We kept on working, and he took the instrument away with him. Later he came back with the same instrument, set it up again, and the apparatus sounded again. I said, "Something's wrong here", so he said, "The machine must be broken". And so he took it away again, came back, and tried to do something with it, so that it didn't start the hooter. But later it did start again. We spent the whole day up there. Some of us felt sick, but we had to go on working. They didn't give us any gas masks. The men from the subcontractors are free to work and free to breathe in the air until it finishes them off. They're not interested. They're only interested in the work being finished off. Nothing else.'

The wearing of safety shoes with steel toecaps is compulsory at Thyssen. So is the wearing of safety helmets. According to the law, Adler should have provided us with these as well as with work gloves. However, Adler makes another saving here. He cheats as much over small matters as over large ones. 'Lots of chickens make muck too' is one of his mottos. When 'people' are in short supply the chargehands and the Thyssen foremen turn a blind eye and even let the new men from Adler work in trainers. There's constant danger in our work, for example from falling debris, from overloaded wheelbarrows overturning, or from passing forklift trucks. I never wore any regulation work shoes with steel toecaps, neither did several other workmates. I was lucky that nothing happened to me.

As for work gloves, we have to look for them in bins and refuse containers. We only find oil-smeared, torn ones, thrown away by Thyssen workers after the company has given them new ones. We have to buy the hard hats ourselves, or perhaps we might be lucky enough to find a damaged one that's been thrown away. German workers' heads are obviously more valuable and more in need of protection than those of immigrants. On two occasions, Zentel tore the helmet off my head, to give it to a German worker who had forgotten his. The first time I protested, 'Wait, I bought, belongs to me,' but Zentel put me in my place: 'Nothing belongs to you here, except maybe some wet shit. You can get it back after the shift.' Here, your property is expropriated just like that, no one bothers to ask. On the second occasion, I was put with a new German, who got his helmet provided free by Remmert, but who, for the moment, was still working without one. Once again, Ali was supposed to risk his head for the German's. This time, I refused. 'Is private, belongs to me. Cannot do. Can get sack, if work without helmet.' The foreman: 'You bloody well give him the helmet, otherwise I'll sack you. And right this minute!' So Ali bowed before force, and worked the whole shift without a helmet, in a section of the slabbing-mill where, only a few yards away, lumps of ore that were still glowing fell to the ground. Had one struck me on the head, I would at the very least have been badly burned.

The German worker took it for granted that his protection would be at my cost. When I put it to him, he only said, 'I can't do anything about it either. I'm only doing what they tell me. Complain to someone else, I'm the wrong person.' Later he also lets Ali feel his contempt: 'You people from Adler are worth nothing. You can't be all there. I wouldn't pick up a shovel for that money.' Which is as much as to say, you have absolutely no rights at all; officially you don't even exist. You have no cards, no contract, nothing. And that's why he looks down on us. As a German working for Remmert, he's privileged. He gets paid overtime and holiday rates and an hourly wage of 11.28 marks, gross. (However, Remmert does not pay any allowances for dirty work, even though most of the jobs involve handling used grease, oil and thick metal dust.) The men from Adler are to do the same work for even less money – how much less remains to be shown.

I rent a tiny one and a half room flat in Diesel Street, in Duisburg. I want to take one step closer to Ali, and really live like a Turkish worker in West Germany, rather than just making daily excursions to the workplaces, as I have been doing up to now. I identify more and more with the part. At night, when I'm asleep, I often talk aloud in broken German. I now know what strength it takes to bear just for a short time, what my foreign colleagues have to suffer all their lives. It's not difficult to find the flat; Bruckhausen is a part of the city that's dying. For years it was almost entirely Turkish, and now many of the Turks have returned to their homeland. Many houses are empty, or in such a bad condition that they are no longer habitable. The flat has neither a sink unit nor a shower, the lavatory in the common hallway is shared by several tenants, and it costs 180 marks per month. Doing it up, I allow myself one great luxury: a friend installs a bath-tub in the middle of the room.

I try to make my new home look a little nicer. I clear two container loads of refuse and debris out of the front garden. The neighbours had unloaded their rubbish here, though nothing they do could make 'the quality of life' in the area any worse. Bruckhausen is right next to the steel mill. Whoever grows old here must have extremely robust health. In every street there are notices with a telephone number to call if the smell gets especially bad. But here, the smell is nearly always especially bad.

Even so, I want to live in Bruckhausen. I'm not quite alone here. Perhaps it will be possible, in summer, to hold an open-air party in my tiny reclaimed garden, with the neighbours or with my workmates . . . .

It's an emergency

There are some workers who go for months without a day off. They live like beasts of burden. They no longer have a private life. They're only allowed to go home because it's cheaper for the company if they pay for their lodgings themselves. Otherwise, it would be more practical if they just slept at Thyssen or Remmert. It's usually the younger ones who do that. Two years at the most in the Thyssen shit and they are worn out, used up, sucked dry, and sick – often for life. For the employers, they're disposable, interchangeable. This fate explains why it's unusual for anyone to stick out the work for more than two years. Often, one or two months are enough to cause irreparable damage to health, especially if double and triple shifts are worked. One workmate, barely 20, regularly works 300 to 350 hours a month.

The Thyssen foremen know it, the company profits by it, and the proof is stamped on the work cards and stored away.

Thyssen often needs the troops from Remmert at very short notice. Sometimes, workers who have been ferried back from Duisburg to Oberhausen after an exhausting shift are fetched out of the showers by the sheriff for another shift. Or people are phoned up and ordered back to work when they've only just fallen asleep in total exhaustion. Most, even the younger and really strong ones, say that it's impossible to stand more than 15 or 16 shifts in a week. Then, if there is the odd free weekend, you sleep through it all dead to the world. Young F. works double shifts nearly every Saturday and Sunday. He does everything, never complains. He crawls into the dirtiest holes without grumbling, scratches wet, hot and stinking layers of grease from the machinery and gets himself covered in slippery oil. He's always somewhat withdrawn, has an aged, smiling face and seldom talks coherently. He is the eldest of 12 children, four of whom have left home. He lives with his parents and seven brothers and sisters in a tiny flat. He's always hungry; if someone doesn't eat his sandwiches, then F. will have them. He only keeps 100 marks of his monthly wage for himself, and hands over the rest to his family, so that they can make ends meet. Whenever anyone is complaining about the work, he objects, 'We should be glad to have any work at all,' and adds, 'I'll do anything'. Once, when a Thyssen supervisor discovered us taking an unauthorized break, he was the only one still working.

He says that his record is 40 hours, with a break of 5 or 6 hours. Only a few weeks ago he worked 24 hours non-stop. He's always looking in bins and containers and collecting the filthy work gloves which Thyssen workers have thrown away. He even keeps single gloves. Some time, he'll find a matching one. He goes on collecting them and has already got quite a pile. I ask him, 'What you do with them? You cannot wear so many gloves.' He says, 'You never know. We don't get any gloves. You should be glad they're lying around. Man, I'll collect anything. You always need another helmet, in case something falls on your head.' I'm sorry for him. He's always smiling. A few weeks later, I'm there when F. is allocated weekend double shifts yet again, but this time he implores the boss, 'I can't any more! I can't, I can't do it.' 'Why, but you've always managed it before!' 'Please, not today. Please, please.' 'I won't forget this. Until now we could always rely on you.' Afterwards, I congratulate him. 'It's good you have said no today, you tired.' He just couldn't take any more. He could hardly walk or stand. His face was ashen and his hands were shaking.

Another worker tells how the previous year they had worked 36 consecutive hours over the Easter weekend. 'Remmert had a contract to clean the paint shop at Opel, in Bochum. The job had to be finished on time, because the new shift was going to clock on at 6 am on the Tuesday after Easter.' However, the marathon shift in the car plant didn't hold the record in terms of hours. 'Two years ago, we worked on a hotel near Frankfurt. The whole team that we went down there with slaved like crazy till we all dropped; we worked for about 50 hours.'

The German worker, Hermann T., about 35, is one of those most eager for work. You can tell just by looking at him. He is greyish-white in the face, very drawn and underweight. He was unemployed for a while, and he's one of the few who really are grateful to be allowed to work till they drop. He's been working like a madman ever since he started in February 1985. According to his own calculations, he did 350 hours in April. In June, he again 'took all the hours going' – by 25 June he'd already worked 300 hours. Hermann T. told me, 'Last week I did four consecutive shifts, from Friday to Saturday. I went into Thyssen at six o'clock on Friday morning and clocked out again at 2.15 pm on Saturday afternoon.' These marathon shifts are nothing unusual for Hermann. To prevent detection of such extreme breaches of the law on working hours, he's ordered to a different job in the giant Thyssen plant for each shift. 'Friday morning, I was at my building site in Ruhrort, just a small hall which we had to drain. Then after lunch I was in Oxy 1; I worked the night shift in the power station at Voerde, and on Saturday morning I was at the building site in Ruhrort again.' Completely exhausted and weak at the knees, he finally staggered home. 'Then I ate something but I wasn't really hungry any more; before I lay down, I told my wife to wake me up at quarter past eight, because I wanted to see the film. But I was out for the count – I slept through till Sunday lunchtime, without waking up once.'

He talks about the work they've done at Thyssen. 'Every day, 16 hours, 12 hours, 13 hours, every Saturday, every Sunday – without a break. We were there at Easter and Whitsun as well, that was crazy. All the blast furnaces were shut down and everything had to be cleaned out. We just slaved, whether there was a gale, whether it was snowing or raining. Your clothes were always damp and wet, there were always 10 or 15 people from Remmert, Adler people as well. We worked for almost five months there.'

Sezer O., a 44-year-old Turkish worker, claims to hold the record for hours worked. During the building of the Munich underground, the workers had to do 72 consecutive hours in an underground shaft, and in their short breaks they often just slept for half an hour where they were. Lots of men had accidents on these marathon jobs, he reports, all of them immigrants.

On one occasion, the sheriff simply forced us – in legal terms it would constitute unlawful duress – to work a double shift. We're just being driven back to the assembly point. We're exhausted. Some of us have already fallen asleep, when the overseer stops our bus and says in an almost offhand manner, 'We keep working! Double shift!'

Some workers protest that they want to go home, that they are totally worn out. The sheriff claims it's Thyssen who demands that the work must go on.

An Algerian worker, T., insists that he has to get back home; he is sacked on the spot. He's pulled off the bus and dumped on the road. It's up to him to make his own way back.

Here, word for word, is the conversation that led up to this:

Boss: 'You've got to work longer today, till ten o'clock.'

Algerian worker: 'Lick my arse! I won't, I'm not a robot!'

Boss: 'You *all* have to work longer.'

Algerian worker: 'I have to go home, it's urgent.'

Boss: 'Then don't bother coming back again. This is an emergency.'

Algerian worker: 'But I must go home.'

Boss: 'Then don't come back tomorrow. Get out. You're finished here. Forever.' The he adds, to the others, who are uneasily silent, 'I need 40 men tomorrow as well! Thyssen insists on it. I'd like to knock off, but no one's asking me either. I've got an appointment for my crowns this afternoon. I won't make it. That's it. What have you got to complain about? In a war, it's all much worse.'

Better to play dumb

During a break in one of the gloomy and deserted long passageways in sintering plant 3, a Thyssen foreman comes towards us, accompanied by a chargehand. They're inspecting how much sludge and slag dust we've cleared away, since the plant can only start running once we've finished. The oriental appearance of Yusuf stimulates the young foreman to revel in holiday memories. 'Are you from Tunisia?' Yusuf answers in the affirmative. The foreman replies, 'A great country. We're going there again this year – me and my wife, on holiday. You can really relax there. And everything's so much cheaper than here.'

Yusuf smiles gratefully at him. It's not often that a German superior condescends to talk to an immigrant about anything apart from work, and rare indeed that he says anything positive about his native country. Yusuf explains that his parents have a house near the sea, mentions the address, and invites the foreman to visit them, the next time he is in Tunisia. The foreman takes him up on it right away. 'Oh, you can be sure I will come. You just have to get me a couple of addresses. You know what I mean. You've got such crazy women to fuck. It's incredible there. How much does it cost at the moment?' Yusuf replies, 'Don't know.' 'Yeah,' continues the foreman, 'you can get everything for a fiver, all in.'

Yusuf's pride is visibly injured, and he replies 'No idea'. But the foreman is in his element now and doesn't let up. He rubs his thumb between his forefinger and middle finger: 'Listen, those are hot women you've got there. Real wildcats. Once you've pulled the veil off, they're real goers. Don't you have a sister? Or is she still too young? With you people, they always have to get married so young.' Yusuf tries to cover up his humiliation in front of the other workers, and says, 'But you will be on holiday with your wife!' The foreman laughs, 'That doesn't matter. She lies on the beach all day and doesn't notice a thing. It's a fantastic hotel. Just like the Intercontinental here. It costs just over 2,000 marks for two weeks. All in. Once we took an excursion to that other country, what's it called?' Yusuf replies politely, 'Morocco'. 'Of course, Morocco, it had just slipped my mind. Lots of fanny there, too. Hey, tell me, what language do you speak? Is it Spanish?' Yusuf can't take it any longer. He turns away, but still manages to be polite. 'No, Arabic. I must go to the toilet.'

The chargehand takes this opportunity to sit down with us and keep up the holiday mood. He stretches. 'Oh to be in the south now. No work. Just sun. And women, women.' Turning to me: 'Is it true that in Anatolia you can buy a woman for a goat?' When I look the other way disinterestedly, he demands, 'It's true, isn't it? How did you get landed with your old dear?'

'The Germans think always, money can buy everything,' I

reply. 'But most beautiful things in world not for money. That's why Germans so poor with all their money.'

The chargehand feels himself attacked, and pays Ali back. 'I wouldn't have one of your Anatolian harem-ladies if you gave me one as a present. They're dirty, they smell. You've got to give them a good scrubbing first. And once you've undressed them, pulled all that stuff off, by that time you're limp again.'

Afterwards, Yusuf takes me aside and says, 'Is not good, that we learned and understand German. Always trouble. Better to play dumb.' He tells me about young Tunisian workers, who because of similar experiences and humiliations have quite deliberately decided not to learn any more German, so that whatever the foreman says, they can always say yes, and then there's no bother.

Many toilets in the Thyssen factory are smeared with racist slogans and invective. Racist grafitti has also been sprayed on the factory walls, but no one feels any need to remove it. Here is an example from the hundreds in the Oxy 1 plant: SHIT ON A STICK = A TURK WITH A WOODEN LEG. And sprayed on a canteen wall nearby: TURKS OUT! GERMANY FOR THE GERMANS!

An animal lover had thoughtfully stuck a sticker beside this, with a picture of a panda and the motto, 'Save threatened species'. Twenty yards further along, in big letters: 'DEATH TO ALL TURKS!' In the toilets of the cold-rolling mill, near the galvanizing section, I noted down a few more slogans. They were faded, so they'd already been there for quite a while:

A THOUSAND RATS IN YOUR BED IS BETTER THAN ONE TURK IN THE CELLAR!
HANG ALL TURKS AND ALL THE GERMAN GIRLS WHO GO WITH THEM!
SHIT TURKS, THEY CAN'T HANG HIGH ENOUGH, I HATE THEM ALL!

TURKISH SWINE, I'LL SHOOT YOU ALL!
I AM PROUD TO BE A GERMAN!
GERMANY FOR THE GERMANS!
AN SS-PIG IS BETTER THAN A TURKISH BASTARD!
THERE NEVER WAS A BETTER GERMAN THAN ADOLF HITLER.

A conversation at work

At break times, underneath the slabbing-mill, the German workers Michael (aged 34), Udo (aged 26), and Alfred (aged 53), who's always got most to say, have got hold of a plank and rested it between two barrels. Here they sit, sharing cigarettes and drinks. Opposite them, on some spread-out pages of the Turkish newspaper, *Hürriyet (Freedom)*, sits Ali. The conversation is constantly interrupted by the noise of lumps of ore thundering down from up above.

Alfred: 'Under Adolf Hitler, if you stole from your workmates you were put against the wall and shot, even if it was only for a shoelace. Believe you me. That's all they're worth; anyone who thieves from a mate – firing squad. That's how it should be. You don't steal from your workmates, you just don't.'

Ali: 'But boss can take away from you?'

Alfred: 'That's completely different, but someone who goes behind his mates' backs or steals . . .'

Ali: 'But boss shot too if he steals?'

Alfred (threat in his voice): 'You should have been here under Hitler, Europe was still all right then.'

Ali: 'Many shot?'

Alfred: 'You should have been here.'

Udo: 'But old people could still walk down the street then.'

Alfred: 'Listen, an old granny of 70 could walk down the street with 10,000 marks in her bag, and nothing would happen to her.'

Ali: 'So much money, she not go down street alone, she drive car . . .'

Alfred: 'In the city, big city – Leipzig, where I come from – my dad had a motorbike, a car and a bicycle. The bike stood in the yard all year long; if it got rusty, then he bought a new one, and it was in the yard again. I was always there . . .'

Ali: 'Must have been junk – that bike.'

Alfred (the way he talks to me, he obviously regards all immigrants as potential thieves): 'Just you sit and listen, and make a note of it between you mutton ears.'

Ali: 'Why?'

Alfred: 'Because of the pinching and thieving that goes on. Listen, people didn't always have automatic washing machines like today. We had a laundry woman, Mrs Müller, because both my parents were working in the family business. Every four weeks there was a big wash, understand? In winter it was dried in the loft, and in summer in the yard. All our washing, starting with the bedlinen, was hung up in the yard. And not a single handkerchief went missing, not a single thing went missing.'

Ali (to the others): 'What I want with his snot-rags? I buy Kleenex.'

Alfred (persevering): 'Not a single handkerchief.'

Ali: 'But for foreigners, not so good then?'

Alfred: 'Just you listen, there was still order and discipline in Germany then.'

Ali: 'But the Jews, you kill them.'

Alfred: 'Fuck your Jews. It was instilled in us, adults must be respected, that was drummed into us. By the teacher, by the school and by our parents. When we were lads we'd never have got away with sitting down in the tram. We got that hammered into us, you stood up for an older person. It was second nature.'

Ali: 'You mean it was better government than now . . .'

Alfred: 'It was total dictatorship, but I felt it was better then than today – better than the pile of shit I'm in today.'

Ali: 'Tell me, why you murder all the Jews?'

Udo (to Alfred): 'Because they were foreigners.'

Alfred: 'Do you know why – do you know why?'

Ali (playing dumb): 'No, no.'

Alfred: 'Hitler made one mistake. He would have had to live another five years, so that none of them would have been left alive, not a single one. Wherever the Jews have got their finger in the pie, there's always trouble, everwhere in the world it's the same, whether it's poor Jews or rich ones. There are rich Jews like Rockefeller, Morgenthau etc. They're the ones who've caused all the mischief and arguments right through history. They've got the money for research, they've got the cash, they've got the power over life and death. And if Hitler had kept going for another five years, and things had somehow turned out right for him, there wouldn't be any more of those people, believe me – not one.'

Ali: 'You kill gypsies too?'

Michael: 'Those who weren't Germans by race, he killed them all, all except racial Germans.'

Udo: 'Yeah, but it wasn't just Hitler!'

Ali: 'He would have killed me too?' (No reply.)

Alfred: 'Come on, who invented concentration camps? Let's have the truth.' He provides the answer himself, loudly. 'The English.'

Udo: 'The Yanks, the Yanks started it.'

Alfred (doggedly): 'It was the English. Churchill, yeah Churchill, was a lieutenant in the English army. Listen, Churchill was in the colonial wars, he was a lieutenant, you know, a sergeant.'

Michael: 'Hitler shouldn't have done that.'

Alfred: 'You know what Churchill did?'

Michael: 'I don't care, it was terrible, it's . . .'

Alfred (interrupts him): He took Southwest Africa away from us, our colonies. And it was him – have you heard of the Boers? He locked women and children up in camps in the desert, and let them all die, women and children – all of them . . .'

Michael: 'That wasn't right, either. But Hitler was the worst mass-murderer of all time . . .'

Alfred (disconcerted because his mate Michael is contradicting him, turns all his aggression on Ali): 'Listen, you're not stupid are you?'

Ali: 'That depends . . .'

Alfred: 'What's the difference between the Turks and the Jews?'

Ali: 'All people, no difference.'

Alfred (triumphant): 'Yes there is. The Jews have got it all behind them.'

Udo puts a word in; he says to Alfred, 'Come on, I know a better one.'

Alfred: 'Spit it out then!'

Udo (to me): 'How many Turks can you fit into a VW?'

Ali: 'I don't know.'

Udo: 'Twenty thousand. You don't believe me?'

Ali: 'Will be right, if you say.'

Udo: 'You want to know how?'

Ali: 'Rather not.'

Udo: 'Easy. Two in front, two in the back, the rest in the ashtray.'

Alfred (drily): 'Ha ha. I can't laugh at that one any more, it's so old. I've heard it at least a hundred times. But have you heard this one? A Turkish boy is taking a German shepherd dog for a walk. He meets this German man, who asks, "Where are you going with that pig?" The Turkish boy says, "That's no pig, that's a genuine German shepherd dog, it's even got a pedigree." "Shut your face," says the man, "I didn't ask you."'

Snorts of laughter from Alfred and Udo.

Michael: 'I don't think it's very funny. Telling that joke with Ali here. He might think you're serious.'

Ali: 'I can't laugh about it. And nothing funny about Jewish joke.' (To Alfred) 'Why the Germans have so little to laugh about that their jokes have to be at cost of others?'

Alfred (angry): 'There's no harm in a joke. Just don't stick your nose into our business, otherwise you'll have nothing to laugh about.' And he asks me provocatively: 'Have you ever heard of Dr Mengele?'

Ali: 'Yes, he was murder-doctor in concentration camp.'

Alfred: 'Ah, Mengele, he wasn't so daft. Anyway, he didn't use any Turks for his experiments. Do you want to know why?'

I prefer to remain silent.

'Because,' he looks at me, filled with hate, 'because you're no use for anything, not even for his experiments.'

Michael: 'But, look, when I see and hear the reports, then I feel ashamed to be a German . . .'

Alfred (with pleasure): 'He put them inside, and then he watched how long they stayed alive in the ice. Listen, what country do you really come from? You're not even a proper Turk, are you? Your mother's a nigger of something, isn't she?

Ali: 'I have Greek mother, Turkish father.'

Alfred: 'So, what are you, Turk or Greek?

Ali: 'Both. And German too. Because already here ten years.'

Alfred (to the others): 'Just listen to this joker. He thinks he's a bit of everything. That's what happens when the races get mixed up. Nobody knows what they are. He doesn't have a country. That's communist. Where he comes from it's all crawling with communists. It should be stopped. Do you know what they did at Mannesmann? Got rid of all the Turks. There are some Turks here at Remmert, you just need to look at them to get angry. You can stick the lot of them in the ovens . . . Like I said yesterday (to a Turkish worker), if you don't do what you're told, I'll kick your arse and send you home. God, I've got my eye on him.'

Michael: 'They worked here, you worked here, we needed you. That's all. You're here now. We're not going to do anything against you.'

Ali: 'We not come by ourselves. We were brought. And always told, "Come! Come! Earn much money here. We need you." We not just arrive.'

Michael: 'Yeah, that's right. We should compensate them.'

Udo: 'Right, that's what Mannesmann are doing.'

Michael: 'There are so many unemployed now, we're in the middle of a crisis.'

Udo: 'Mannesmann said right, 10 to 30,000 marks for each man.'

Ali: 'Only, if all go now, you get no more pension, whole pension system kaput. It we all go, we get money back, and you have no pension.'

Alfred: 'That's all crap. There aren't that many Turks here.'

Ali: 'Yes, one and half million. They you go bankrupt.'

Alfred: 'Do you know what they do in Switzerland? I you're a guest worker in Switzerland, then your job contract runs 11 months; the twelfth month is a holiday month. And during that month when you're at home, you get a letter telling you if you can work again or if you've got to stay home. That's how the Swiss do it. In that month they decide whether you're allowed to come again or whether you have to spend the rest of your life as a camel driver.'

Mehmet's odyssey

I'm often struck by the calm manner of Mehmet, an older worker. With stoical patience, he takes on the hardest and most dangerous jobs. He is friendly, and with his grey hair and round, wrinkled face, looks quite fatherly. I'm a little shocked when Klaus, another Remmert man, tells me that Mehmet is only just 49. I had taken him for 60.

One day, Mehmet leaves for 'five weeks' holiday' in Turkey. I ask other workmates, 'Much holiday at Remmert? Ask Adler for five weeks' holiday, right away sack.' 'Normally, we don't get it either,' says one, 'but Mehmet had three accidents in one year. So, for once, the old man was generous.' I ask further questions. All tell of the serious injuries Mehmet had suffered. The first accident hadn't even happened at Thyssen, but in Remmert's millionaire villa in Mülheim. Mehmet and a German worker were sent to install a sauna in the cellar. Earth had to be excavated, and walls partially removed. 'That's where it happened. The German was digging underneath, and Mehmet noticed that a wall was giving way. He managed to pull out his workmate, who might otherwise have been dead, but Mehmet himself got the falling masonry full on his left shoulder.' The splintered bones were X-rayed, and the doctor certified that Mehmet had a 46 per cent serious disability.

Mehmet had to stay in hospital for more than two months. He didn't receive compensation or a pension from Remmert. Instead, Remmert, dealer in men, promised him that despite the serious injury, he could go on working at Thyssen. In February, Mehmet started work again on the nightshift, in icy cold and during a smog warning. In the sintering plant, he slipped on the ice. Instinctively he tried to break the fall with his healthy arm. As a result, he dislocated his shoulder so badly that it had to be put in plaster. Mehmet, who has to provide for a wife and three children, one of whom is severely handicapped from birth, is only partly recovered when he goes back to work nights. After fourteen consecutive night shifts, Mehmet goes home and falls into bed, utterly exhausted. Two hours later, he's rung up and told to start a day shift. He reports for work. When he wants to clock off at 8 pm in the evening, the chargehand orders him to come back again right away after eating, for the next night shift. Mehmet reports for work once more.

In a basement vault, Mehmet starts to clean out channels into which glowing iron is constantly falling; the iron is producing such thick steam that he can't see his hand in front of his face any more. Over-exhausted, his leg slips into a hole. The diagnosis at hospital is that his ligaments are torn. But even after two operations, his leg has still not fully recovered. Despite his bad leg, he keeps on working.

On Mehmet's return from holiday he says to me, 'What should I do? Must do work. Children, debts . . .' It's difficult to engage him in conversation. After only a few days back, he is already completely overworked and fatigued again. Time, for him, consists only of shifts; he hardly remembers individual months any more, only whether it was especially cold or dirty at Thyssen. Although he has been in West Germany since 1960, he only speaks very broken German. The struggle to survive has not even left him enough time to learn the language properly (a Turkish colleague helped me to translate what he said). Anyway, he isn't asked to chat in his job, only to put his back into the work.

With incredible effort, Mehmet has tried to do something that counts as a virtue in Germany, for Germans, that is: to establish a home for himself and his family. He tells me that during his first ten years in Germany, he worked anywhere he could find a job, from one end of the country to the other. Finally, in 1970, he succeeded in getting a permanent job at Thyssen in Duisburg, as a forklift driver. 'I earned 1,600 to 1,700 marks take-home pay. I also had a part-time job on the side doing car upholstery . . .'

After saving for years, and with the help of bank loans, Mehmet bought himself and his family a dilapidated terrace house in Duisburg-Mettmann. 'If I had kept Thyssen job, everything would be paid now.' But his German chargehand thwarted these modest calculations. 'I was about to go on holiday in 1980. the chargehand comes, says to all Turks: "Bring me back a carpet from Turkey, but a genuine one!" So I said, listen, genuine carpet at home costs minimum 5,000 marks, for good quality. I don't have that much money. So he says, "If you don't bring me one, you'll be in for it when you get back!" ' When Mehmet came back from Turkey, the chargehand victimized him for days with heavy jobs, as 'punishment' for the missing 'present'. 'Then he said, "Come to my office!" So I went to his office, he shouted a bit, I didn't say anything. Then three hours later, I was working again, company security men come, take me, tell me to go home, because I had hit chargehand. But that wasn't true at all.' After ten years at Thyssen, Mehmet was dismissed without notice, and without a thorough examination of the case. In fact, there wasn't even a charge against him. But because of the reason given by Thyssen in the dismissal notice ('physical attack on another employee'), the employment office at first refused benefit. Mehmet had to present witnesses. A number of workmates, including Germans, were unanimous in their statements to the employment office that the grounds for dismissal were quite obviously fabricated. Mehmet says, 'That was all a real shock. Then I went looking and looking to find new work. Found nothing for two or three months. Then, eventually, a job at chipboard company, Duisburg-Homberg. Again as forklift driver. I was there five months, was all OK, no problem. Then I got a telegram which said that my mother had died. Went to the boss, asked if I could have a week off to go the funeral. He said, "Why, we don't give holidays after only five months!" I said, "But my mama is dead". He only said, doesn't interest him. So I went anyway and came back a week later – dismissal.' Under the pressure of the debts for his little house, Mehmet looked for a new job – unsuccessfully. Another three months' unemployment. 'Then I took a driving test, class two, for vans, applied everywhere. At last I get a job driving delivery vans for a little company, not much money. After two days, a letter comes from the Rheinperle company. I had once repaired tarpaulin there for the vans. Went there, boss says: "You can start with us right away, driving forklifts, later perhaps lorries." I stayed four years.' An 'even better' offer tempted Mehmet to change companies: 13 marks an hour with a Düsseldorf removal business. 'Plus 18 marks expenses; I took it right away, of course.' But after only five months came the dismissal; the reason, 'lack of work'.

'So I started running around again. Employment office says come again in three months or four, there's no work. Again asking at companies everywhere. Then a neighbour tells me Remmert needs drivers. I ask, "Where is Remmert?" He says, "Ask at Mannesmann". I go to Manesmann. One week long, every day, I waited for the boss of the Remmert people. But he didn't come. Every day to Gate 4, waiting. Then a welder tells me, office is in Oberhausen. Immediately, I go to Oberhausen, in the afternoon, three or four o' clock. Ganger only says, can start right away, we do a lot of heavy work, always lots of dirt. I say, I like working, don't care if it's heavy or dirty, must work. Earn bread, I must.'

Remmert pays 12.24 marks an hour; Mehmet pays with his health.

And elsewhere . . .

Adler would like to be 'as big as Remmert' one day. That's his dream. The distance between an Adler and a Remmert is not very great. The difference is like that between twilight and darkness. While Adler sells his people without any official authorization at all, Remmert sometimes operates legally.

The company owner, Alfred Remmert, has done so well that now he hardly needs to do more than count the money that his two companies 'pull in' by renting out workers. Some 170 people are employed in his firm, Industrial Cleaning Ltd, to whom Adler, in turn, sells labour, and he has another 660 men and women working for him in his office cleaning company, SWI.

Even for the extremely heavy work at Thyssen or Mannesmann, which is comparable to demolition or building work, Remmert only pays wages at the rate for office cleaners:

11.28 marks an hour. Anyone who stands the work for more than a year receives 60 pfennigs extra. The normal rate for building workers would be 14.09 marks.

A Turk who was working for Remmert at Mannesmann, reports that the manager made promises that weren't kept, to encourage workers to achieve higher productivity. 'We were told, if you burn more than 20 tons a day, then we'll pay another 2 marks for every additional ton. We put in an extra effort, and by the end of the week, we had burned an extra 1,600 tons; that would have been 3,200 marks. For each burner, there were eight Turks and three Germans, that added up to 300 marks each. But Remmert didn't pay us a single penny more.'

Yilmaz G. adds, 'Our mates, who as Remmert men were working in the coke works, were also dissatisfied with their wages, because a lot of men there from other firms were getting more money for the same work. There were people there from a demolition company in Duisburg; they were getting as much as 3.50 marks per hour more.'

At Mannesmann, just as at Thyssen, extra hours are constantly required. Yilmaz estimates the monthly average of the Remmert workers at Mannesmann as between 230 and 250 hours.

At Mannesmann, too, the workers are pushed around and treated like convicts, and here too there are dust and gases; everywhere, there is the risk of an accident. A shop steward at Mannesmann explains: 'For example, someone who is employed as a burner in the blast furnaces works all day in an unnatural, stooping position. In addition, there's the constant heat.' 'It's almost like the galley ships used to be,' says Ali K. 'If you can't keep up, they throw you overboard. We had a Turkish colleague, who was working for Remmert as a burner at Mannesmann. One day, he was struck across the knees by a chain while loading iron – both his legs were broken. He had to stay in hospital for six or seven months and after a short while Remmert sacked him.

After he had recovered a bit, he turned up at the factory one day and asked if he could work a four or five hour shift, because after the accident he couldn't stay on his feet so much any more. The manager didn't even let him finish; he just sent him away.'

The frequent double and triple shifts Remmert demands make accidents inevitable. For example, the Remmert company removes slag in the steel mill in trucks. Colleagues report that men have been driving these trucks and trailers non-stop for up to 36 hours. That's not only a dangerous risk for the Remmert people themselves, but also for everyone who uses the factory's internal roads. 'If someone taking those corners has been driving for 36 hours, then it's only a question of time before there's a serious accident,' reckons Ali K.

The Duisburg company, Staschel, another labour contractor on the Mannesmann site, had its workers do one shift in the morning at the coke works, one in the afternoon at the steel mill, and in the evening a night shift in a subsidiary tubing plant in Mülheim. The men worked for 24 hours non-stop.

At Mannesmann, the slave trade began after the company had forced Turkish and other foreign permanent workers out of the factory. In order to get rid of them, Mannesmann offered up to 40,000 marks 'resettlement aid'. They wanted to reduce the workforce by 600. At the same time, the company management fanned the German workers' fears that their jobs were at risk if not enough foreigners returned home. This threat produced an extremely tense atmosphere in the plant. Many German workers wanted the Turks to disappear, so that, for example, their own sons, who were doing apprenticeships in the company, could take their places. Older Turks had to take a German language test, which was an attempt to demonstrate their lack of suitability. Those who still didn't show themselves 'willing to return' were put under pressure by the prospect of short-time working and dismissal under a 'compensation plan'. A thousand Turks ended up leaving Mannesmann. This was the signal for subcontractors like Remmert to fill the gap.

The suspect

'All the Adler people over here!' During a break, the sheriff claps his hands and summons us over to him. 'I want you all to know that Mr Adler wants to meet you at four o'clock after work today, in the 'Sportlereck' pub, Skagerrack Street, to talk to you about conditions of work and your constant money demands. You must be punctual, because he hasn't got much time, I can tell you that.'

The meeting takes place in our own unpaid free time. After we've sat around for more than an hour after work, we make our way to the pub. We wait a quarter of an hour, we wait half an hour; Adler doesn't show up. 'He's only fucking us around,' says Mehmet, 'let's go home.' The only ones to stay on are Adler's faithful ganger, Wormland, his brother Fritz, aged 23, and myself.

We're standing at the bar when three policeman, two in uniform, one in plain clothes, enter the pub and look round, scrutinizing the 20 or so customers. One of them asks, 'Has anyone just come in, about 40, blond, five foot six tall? The Commercial Bank round the corner has been raided, and 40,000 marks stolen.'

Sniggers from my German neighbour at the bar, a man of about 60, who's on his eighth beer. 'I wouldn't give him away, wouldn't tell anybody if I knew,' he says, loud enough for the police to hear. 'If he went 50–50 with me, I'd keep quiet all right.' 'Who's the owner of the green VW-Passat with Cologne number plates outside?' the oldest of the policemen asks sternly. I look through the window and see that a police van is parked immediately in front of my battered, rusty car, and that several policemen are looking at it with curiosity. Hell, if they identify me now, my whole plan will be exposed. I had taken the precaution of changing the name in which the car was registered, but I don't have any false documents on me.

My car really does look pretty dilapidated; for me, a car is simply a useful object, a means of getting around, not an item of conspicuous consumption, and so it seems to fit the police clichés: someone driving a car like that obviously needs to rob a bank.

I don't react, and look the other way. My German workmate, Fritz, nudges me and says, 'Hey, that's your car, why don't you tell them?!' 'Shut up,' I tell him, 'the car hasn't got its MOT.' Quick as a flash, Fritz turns Ali's predicament to his own advantage. 'What do I get if I keep quiet? A 100 marks or I'll tell them!' He looks over at the policemen. 'I don't have that much,' I say, and beat him down to a crate of beer.

Meanwhile, the police have begun to question each of the customers, to find out to whom the suspicious car belongs, and one approaches our table. We can't help him either. The police disappear. I breathe freely again, and am thinking I've managed to get away with it, when a new group of police appears – three in uniform this time and two in plain clothes. A badly organized search operation, in which one hand doesn't know what the other's doing, seems to be underway because the officer in charge puts the same question as his colleague: whether a man, about 40, blond, about five foot six tall, had come in with a white plastic bag containing notes to the value of 40,000 marks. Some of the customers start laughing, taking the whole thing as a joke. 'Yeah, he's just gone for a pee, but he'll be back in a minute,' says a 40-year-old man who could easily fit the police description of the culprit. 'We can do without the nonsense, please!' The officer can't take a joke. 'Or I'll take you in for giving misleading information and obstructing our inquiries.'

His eyes scan the customers in the bar and come to rest on me. I am the only foreigner in the pub, my working clothes look somewhat shabby; the black streaks of oil on my face haven't quite come off. 'You, come with us,' the officer in charge points at me, and his two younger subordinates approach me, thirsty for action. I feel quite weak as I envisage being found out and my work coming to nothing. For just a moment, I consider running out past them and seeking my safety in flight. But the streets outside are full of policemen, and some trigger-happy marksman could easily shoot me in the back. Stay quite calm, I tell myself, just don't look nervous, the law's completely on my side. What can they pin on me? 'Why take me?' I say, on the offensive right away. 'Am young man, 28 and five foot nine and black hair. Thief is older and smaller.' I point out the obvious dissimilarity. The officer isn't interested in logic. Inspired by me, he thinks he's hot on the trail of something. 'Come with us,' he orders bluntly, 'just speak when you're asked to.' One of his associates tries to grab me by the arm, but I shake him off, and say, 'Doing nothing, I'm coming.'

In front of the pub, other policemen, some in plain clothes, surround me. Bloody hell, how am I going to get out of this? They're frustrated because the real culprit has slipped through their fingers and now they need a substitute victim. 'Show your identity papers,' says the officer. 'Don't have,' I say, 'Boss Adler take away from us, every day work at Thyssen and not get money.' I try to create some confusion, in order to divert attention away from myself. But he doesn't take it up. 'Name? Where do you live?' he interrogates me.

I carefully spell out my Turkish name, S-i-n-i-r-l-i-o-g-l-u, and smile at him, as he curses at its difficulty. I try to encourage him, 'I know, difficult name. Just call me Ali.' It doesn't seem to appease him at all, and his face assumes an even grimmer expression. I tell him my address, Diesel Street 10, where, however, I am not yet officially registered. Confirmation that no Ali Sinirlioglu is registered there promptly comes over the radio. The younger policeman takes me by the arm again; 'Then we'll drive to your house, and you can show us your ID there.' Again,

I go on the offensive. 'Boss has ID, just coming. He is big gangster, steals our money, belongs in prison, should take him.' And I try to draw attention to Thyssen again. 'Can come with me, Gate 20, my card there, can see that I work there.' They're somewhat annoyed, but haven't the faintest intention of taking a closer look at Ali's boss, even though everything about him stinks. The connection with the name of Thyssen doesn't interest them. It seems that they don't want to burn their fingers.

A policeman makes a suggestion to the officer in charge. 'The best thing is to take him to the bank and confront him with the witnesses.' 'Yes, wonderful, with pleasure,' I immediately agree with enthusiasm, and start to climb into the patrol car in my oily work clothes. The commander pulls me back and shouts, 'Out! You'll muck up all the seats with your grease.' Meanwhile a small crowd of people has formed around us. 'He tried to assault a German girl,' rages a housewife of about 50 with a bursting shopping bag which she has propped against the wall behind her.

'What cold, piercing eyes he has,' a 60-year-old man agrees, 'that's what lunatics who run amok look like.' A younger man in his 20's, leaning against his bicycle, corrects them, 'No, he's only robbed the bank.' An argument breaks out. The majority agree with the young man; others, however, insist on the rape theory. One even claims to have heard the assaulted girl 'screaming' as she was 'taken away in the ambulance'.

I'm interrogated in the street for about 20 minutes, during which time the real bank robber has no doubt been able to escape at his leisure, until the commanding officer reaches a decision. 'You go back into the pub and wait until we return with the witnesses. Don't try to leave. A police officer will remain at the door to make sure that you don't try to make a run for it.' I wait for almost an hour but no witnesses arrive. Afterwards, the police themselves must have been struck by the absurdity of suspecting me and presumably didn't want to look foolish in front of the witnesses. Once the police guard disappeared, I sneaked away to my car and, extremely relieved, drove off.

Before that, I turn to the German customers in the pub. 'Did you get that? Only because I foreigner, had to go. The real man was blond, only five six, and older.'

'Well, you could always have popped on a wig,' a 50-year-old at the bar jokes, and the whole pub snorts and hoots with laughter. The man, who is a local authority tax officer, confides in me, 'I followed from what was happening outside that your lot are working black at the steel mill. You're not the only ones. We're always getting to hear about it, but my bosses still wouldn't ever take the issue up, even if I were to report it to them now.'

Three months later, I have a second brush with the police. I come away from Adler, pretty tired, get into my car, which is parked a couple of streets away, and reverse into a brand new VW-Golf.

In seconds, a small crowd has formed around Ali. The owner of the car comes up, upset, and Ali explains to her it was his fault. He immediately wants to take responsibility for the damage and put it in writing as well. In the background, some Germans, who are completely uninvolved, shout out, 'Don't believe him, he's a foreigner, he'll cheat you. Call the police right away.'

All I have with me is a driving licence made out for a Turkish worker, who doesn't in the slightest resemble Ali. To be identified by the police in this way would be an all too banal and trivial conclusion to my efforts. So Ali pleads with the woman, 'Please, not police. Already have endorsements. Maybe sentence, perhaps driving licence taken, maybe even deportation back to Turkey.' The woman hesitates, but someone in the crowd, which unanimously takes the view that 'the police should be here', has already hurried over to the shop across the road to call the police.

An older policeman soon appears, looks at me with considerable suspicion, takes down the details of the accident, and requests me to come with him to the nearby police station. 'If there's anything on him, we'll inform you right away,' he reassures the woman. He compares the photo on the driving licence with me, and nods, as if to say, yes, that's the same person, although there's no similarity at all. He checks the other information by computer and seems surprised when nothing negative is registered. 'There's nothing against you, you can go,' he dismisses me.

'Good work,' I congratulate him, 'in Turkey takes two days.'

'Well, we're in Germany,' he informs me, not without pride.

'Have noticed,' I reply, 'but best wishes.' I'm pleased as punch to be outside again.

The railings

Adler has something quite different for me for a change. 'Turn up at 7 o'clock tomorrow morning at Theo Remmert's company. He's the brother of our Remmert. You'll be painting railings on piecework. 'How much work is there?' Ali want to know, and 'How long?' 'Oh, plenty,' replies Adler, 'it could last a year.' 'And the pay?' When I ask such an irrelevant question, Adler is put in a corner. He pretends to be working it out and comes up with, 'Well, let's say a mark a metre.'

The foreman in the factory, to whom I have to report next morning, is expecting me. With a gentle smile, he hears that Adler has sent me and asks about the wages agreed on. When he hears that it's one mark per metre he says, 'You'll have to keep at it damned hard if you want to earn anything. You can't afford to have breaks.' It appears that the firm of Remmert is under pressure to meet its delivery date. The finished railings were supposed to be delivered to a new plant at Ruhr chemicals and erected almost immediately.

It was all-out slaving for nearly a week. If I work from morning to night with no more than a ten-minute break, the most I can do is 50 metres a day. The railings are 1.25 metres high; three round bars have to be painted with a brush and underneath there's also a large bar. You have to use a small brush to get into every crack and corner. Then the rails have to be moved with a crane to another corner of the hall, and brought back again finished. Nobody paid Ali for that time. Neither is he paid when the foreman comes and says that some of the railings have not been painted carefully enough, that paint is missing in a few tiny places. This means moving the heavy objects backwards and forwards by crane again.

I try to work with two brushes at once to save time. But it doesn't save much. A German, who has a regular job with Remmert and had painted railings on hourly pay, looks at me sympathetically and says: 'No one can keep up that pace all day long. You'll crack up. Give yourself time.' When he hears what the piecework rate is, he shakes his head. 'I'd throw it in their faces. I wouldn't paint a stroke for that.' He openly admitted that he managed, at most, half as much work as Ali and received 13 marks an hour for it. Ali's rate of work produced about 5 to 7 marks an hour.

In spite of the miserable wages, when you are on piecework you develop a completely different attitude to working. You are under continual stress, but the pressure is different. There's no one standing behind you all the time. You're not worried about foremen and supervisors. So you do the work with a much better feeling than at Thyssen. Even if you come home completely done in. When you look at the clock you are shocked that it is so late. At Thyssen it's exactly the opposite; the hours drag, and you're damned glad when they're over. You count each one and are fed up if you look at the clock and there are still four endless, painful hours to go before the end of the shift. Yet piecework is the lowest, most harassed form of independence without any of the advantages that should go with it.

Every day, the Remmert foreman checks my daily quota and takes the work away. Sometimes I have to redo some parts or rub down lumps which have formed and paint them over. When I tell the foreman that I can't manage on my wages and that I feel myself completely abused on 5 or 6 marks an hour, he waves me away: 'It's nothing to do with us. We pay Adler. He gets a good price for it. You must ask him.' He would not let on how much profit Adler was making in his case. I estimate that he's getting at least three to five times what I'm getting, just for supplying the slave labour, and without lifting a finger himself.

After I have painted 210 metres of railings front, back, above and below with ochre paint (and my shoes, trousers and shirt with them), the job is finished. The foreman explains that the railings I have painted will be put up by Remmert's workmen in a new Ruhr chemicals plant. But it'll be a few weeks before any new railings are welded together.

So much for Adler's promise of a year's work. When I explain the situation to him on the telephone, he tells me, 'Never mind. Turn up at five tomorrow morning ready to work for Thyssen again.' And when Ali asks about payment for the railings he says, 'We'll reckon up as soon as I've been given my money by Remmert.' And, 'At the weekends you can always go and paint more railings.'

When, after three weeks, I still haven't been paid my 210 marks for the hard work on the railings, I speak to Adler again. 'You did not paint the railings properly,' he claims, and, 'I can't pay you because you have got me into great trouble and I'm not getting my money.' When I ask why, he mutters about the 'my-count' being wrong, meaning that the paint was not the correct thickness. I think it's one of his usual tricks, but even if it is true, it's not my fault. The Remmert foreman had inspected my work and had accepted it. So Ali sets out to demand his money personally from Mr Remmert. In order to give him a

fright, I go to Theo Remmert's office building straight after the
Thyssen shift, still wearing my work clothes and with my face all
black and filthy. In the entrance hall downstairs the life's
wisdom of the owner, Mr Theo Remmert, is framed on the wall:

> **There are people who think the boss is a mangy
> wolf that should be killed. Others think the
> boss is a cow that can be continually milked.
> Only a few see him as the man who pulls the
> cart.**

Ali, swallower of dust, ironblacker, loadbearer and coolie
makes his way to Remmert the cartpuller and proverbsmith. He
manages to slip past the women at reception and reach the
management floor. Remmert himself is out, but one of his
directors is talking on the telephone about a deal involving
millions. His mouth drops when he sees me come in. 'What's
this moo?' I ask him. 'Did my work, foreman say OK, and now
no money.' 'You mean "my", that's the paint thickness,' the
director corrects me. 'I don't know anything about it, go to
Adler, he should give you your money.'

This crazy game goes on. Adler sends Ali to Ruhr chemicals to
'paint over', as he puts it: 'Otherwise no money.' Ali searches for
hours round the sprawling, stinking Ruhr chemicals plant on the
edge of Oberhausen, until he eventually finds his railings firmly
erected at a dizzy height on a steel frame structure. He wants to
climb up, but a supervisor holds him back. 'You'll kill yourself.
The climbing bars have still to be fitted.' He knows nothing
about 'moo' or 'my'. 'It doesn't make any fucking difference,' he
says. 'The thing is, the railings have been put up, and they're not
going to fall down again.' So Ali complains to Adler by phone:
'Ali again. Foreman say moo not matter. Railings hold up and
cannot fall down.' Adler bursts out: 'First paint them over, go
there again next week, otherwise no money.'

The next visit to Ruhr chemicals doesn't get any results either. If I had really repainted the erected railings, my hourly pay would have dropped to 2 marks an hour, because having to climb up and down would have made the job take much longer. As usual, in the end, Ali didn't get a penny for this special job. And it was tough work. Altogether his railings could have fenced half a football pitch.

The wild west

We have to make tremendous efforts to get at least a part of our wages.

Adler lives in a well-kept, pretty suburb of Oberhausen, about 9 miles from the Thyssen steel mill, where the industrial pollution is filtered by a nearby belt of woodland. The bus journey from the grey, dirty working-class districts to Adler's home requires changing several times and the buses are not that frequent. The workers have got to put up with the waiting. Often enough, someone who has made an appointment with Adler by phone, ends up finding the front door of Adler's house firmly shut. It's often better to stalk him and take him by surprise, and to stand and ring the bell so that he can't see from the window who it is. Adler always has the same standard phrases for getting rid of his men: 'I've got no way of checking that now,' or 'I'm not going to fuck anyone about over an hour here or there,' or 'I don't have my cheque book here, and I certainly don't have any cash,' or 'I've been trying to get hold of you for days. The wage slip will be ready on Monday' (it isn't of course), or 'My proper office is in Dinslaken. I've got a steel construction company there. All the stuff's there.' So he makes an appointment for the following day, and doesn't turn up. Or he says to me: 'If things keep going as well as this, then I'm sure to raise your pay by another mark or so. You can count on it. We'll talk about it again next month.' But there's never a rise.

Instead of increasing the wage, as promised, by one mark, two months later he cuts Ali's wage by a mark. He explains why he won't pay any overtime bonus, even if Easter, Whitsun and Christmas are worked. 'It's because we work more cheaply. That's why Thyssen uses small or medium-sized companies like us, because as a rule we can work more cheaply than their own people. That's the only reason they do it! They would prefer to sack even more Thyssen workers and bring in more companies like us, because companies like this are cheaper.' He recommends tricks which will present an appearance of legality for the authorities. 'Part-time work certificates! There's a law which allows you to earn up to 390 marks a month tax free, and then if you can produce a relative as well, who'll let you use his name, then that's already 780 marks, net, on part-time. And that's completely legal.'

Another thing he does is to register someone who's fallen ill retroactively, at the Health Insurance office. And then there's his method for avoiding long overdue wages payments; he constantly demands 'a record of hours worked, signed by foreman Zentel, otherwise there's no money because I can't check anything!' It's my impression that he's arranged this little game with Zentel, who, as a rule, refuses to sign such slips. 'I've no time for that,' he usually claims. 'Adler gets the exact number of hours each one of you has worked every day anyway.' So we often run back and forward without getting the slips and without getting our wages. Although work times are also registered on our Thyssen clock cards, Adler is not impressed. 'I'm not interested. As far as I'm concerned, the clocking-on cards don't prove anything.'

I go to Adler, unannounced, with Osman; we take the precaution of not arriving till 6.30 pm, to make sure we actually find him at home. It's Osman's last day in West Germany. He has given up, and is finally going back to Turkey by bus the next day. He had already made the journey out to Adler the day before, but even with an appointment, he had not seen him.

When Adler sees me, he's appalled. 'What a sight you are! You look terrible.' 'Yeah, work like that. Always dirt and dust, must make clean, but not go away with washing. Is too much dirt, go under skin.' Adler is more worried about his wallpaper and says: 'Come away from my white wall, stand at least a yard away from it, otherwise you'll lean on it. You're swaying around, you're so tired.' He shouts at Osman: 'You just arrive on my doorstep! What a bloody nerve! Come wandering up here at seven o'clock in the evening! Osman says, 'But I'm going back to Turkey in the morning and wanted to buy something. I've got no money at all.' Adler tells him, 'I can't do anything about it. What an almighty cheek!' He can't control himself any more, and on this occasion his indignation is for real. He repeats himself at least three times (What cheek!), becoming more outraged each time. 'Next you'll be turning up here at ten or eleven at night!' 'No, no, not worry,' I say, 'not so late, must sleep sometime.' But Adler won't let himself be calmed down. 'What a cheek you've got! Fucking come up to my house at seven o'clock. You've got a nerve. Don't try it again. You can't fuck around with me. Going to Turkey tomorrow. That's a lie too. Just don't try to lie to me.' 'Is right,' I say, 'I take him to bus.' Adler shouts at me, 'What's it got to do with you? Just keep your nose out of it! They come to your house at seven o'clock, at quarter past seven. This isn't the wild west you know!'

Osman doesn't give up. 'But, Mr Adler, what am I supposed to do? Tomorrow, I'm not here any more, and I'll have worked for almost nothing.'

'I too,' I add, 'no money for weeks. Give something to eat.'

Adler exclaims, 'You think I'm going to just spit it up for you? Out you go! You people are nothing but a nuisance!'

Outside in the street, tears fill Osman's eyes. 'He's cheated me out of my money. Now I'm going back to Turkey forever, and I can't do anything about it.'

Yüksel's anger

Back at Thyssen again. Conversation with Yüksel Atasayar, 20, after work. We're waiting for our transport to come, exhausted, with dust in every pore.

Yüksel: 'I spend 30 to 40 marks a week on lotto, but not always.'*

Ali: 'In one week?'

Yüksel: 'Sometime perhaps I'll be lucky. It's better to spend 30 to 40 marks on that than on cigarettes. Just think, Cigarettes every day. In a month? Work it out: 4 marks times 30.'

Ali: 'Yes, 120 marks. 1,440 in a year. 14,000 in ten years, and then if you add interest, you have in 20 years almost 30–40,000 marks.'

Yüksel: 'Nice, too . . . If we're still alive in 20 years.'

Ali: 'Not if we do this shit. You can be gone in two years. Get cancer. Does not always come right away, sometimes only five years later.'

Yüksel: 'Yeah, first the pain and everything, and then you're dead. At least you can try to save a little, and then spend it all before you die. If I have the guts, I'll do myself in one day. How long do you want to live? What a load of shit! Do you believe in God?'

Ali: 'No, In us, not outside. You cannot count on it, He will not help you.'

Yüksel: 'If there is a God, why has He made Adler?'

Ali: 'Faulty model. Wanted something quite different, turned out wrong.'

Yüksel: 'If there is a God, He doesn't make mistakes. God is God. He isn't allowed to make any mistakes, He can't make any mistakes.'

Ali: 'Maybe a screwy one, a mad one. Went off head sometime.

---

* A gambling game with weekly coupons like the football pools.

Otherwise no Adler and not this shitty work here.'

Yüksel: 'God, I'm sick of it all!'

Twenty-year-old Yüksel is one of the most careful observers amongst the Turkish workers. He knows which of the Germans are prejudiced against Turks even if they don't say so openly. He knows the daily moods of the German gangers and chargehands, and warns his friends in advance of their whims and bullying. 'Watch out, Zentel is looking for a victim today,' he says at the yard in the morning, while the sheriff is still napping in his Mercedes. He spots the signs of an approaching storm. And, a few hours later Zentel does, in fact, blow up, and sends a Turkish worker home because he's dared to leave the workplace during the unpaid break, and so missed Zentel's inspection.

Yüksel is Turkish in name only. He grew up in Germany, speaks German without an accent, and feels himself to be a German. His appearance doesn't at all correspond to the cliché of what a Turk looks like. He has dark blond hair and blue-grey eyes. His father is of Russian origin. Only his name puts him amongst the Turkish workers, whom he has difficulty in understanding. If he had a German name he would probably not attract the hatred of Alfred, the ganger, who constantly finds excuses for venting his aggression on Yüksel and the other immigrants.

When, on one occasion, Yüksel dares to remind Alfred, who is working like a madman again, and has completely forgotten the time, that, in fact, the break has started, Alfred plants himself in front of him and shouts: 'First the job gets finished, and then there's a break. That's how it used to be in Germany. That's what we were taught. And do you know what you are? You are a giant arsehole, an arsehole.' During the break, Alfred's anger rises again, culminating in a new attack of rage. 'If you ever meet Mengele, you know who that is, he was one of our best "medical researchers", he's still alive, they couldn't get him. If he's standing at the ramp and you come past, then I guarantee he'll tell you: "Off to the right! Off to be gassed! You're no use for any experiments." And do you know why?' Yüksel is quite pale and doesn't dare talk back. He only says, 'No, why?' 'Because you're no use for anything. You only came here to avoid the military dictatorship, to grow up in German kindergartens, to be fattened up here. If you had stayed there, you would have learned what it means to live decently. You Turks have never had a democracy. You don't even know what it's like. First, you've got to learn to live with the military dictatorship and not piss around at our expense.'

Yüksel has given up defending himself against these outbreaks. He knows from experience how little it takes for words to become blows. He prefers to go out of the way of further abuse, picks up his sandwiches without a word, and sits down out of sight, out of earshot, in a distant corner of the factory hall. When he reappears 15 minutes later, there are light, smudged streaks on his dust-blackened face.

Yüksel is also the only person who notices that I often make notes during short breaks. Sometimes he winks at me as if to show that I have his approval. Nevertheless, it unsettles me and makes me nervous. I don't know if he will end up talking to other workers about it.

One day, after especially arduous, hot work near the blast furnaces, as we're sitting on the ground in front of the factory wall, exhausted, waiting for the minibus to pick us up, he asks me, 'Are you writing everything down?' 'Please, don't say a word to anyone.' I take advantage of the opportunity to tell him: 'I can't talk about it yet, but you'll learn all about it later.'

He realizes how worried I am, and how seriously I take it, and doesn't ask any further questions. He doesn't let a word escape during all the months I'm there. 'You must note it all carefully,' he whispers to me. 'Absolutely everything that these bastards make us do. Get it all down!' He seems to have an idea of what I'm planning, and passes on useful information, without wanting to know anything more from me. He's not very political, he's still almost a child, but he keeps the secret, moved by a deep feeling of humiliation and despair, and the sense of solidarity that comes from it.

Yüksel describes his situation like this: 'When my parents came to Germany 20 years ago, I had just been born. We come from Amasia. Where that actually is, I'm not quite sure. Near Armenia, anyway, but I don't really know exactly, to tell the truth. At home we speak Turkish. But I can't really speak it very well. I couldn't keep up with a proper discussion. I can't really follow newspapers in Turkish either. But my parents speak perfect Turkish and they speak only Turkish to one another. They don't speak German well. I feel more of a German than a Turk.

'My father is employed full time at Thyssen, in the lathe-rolling shop. He doesn't earn much. 1,200 to 1,300 marks a month.

'How did I get a job here? Well, another worker told me about it. I just asked the foreman. I had been told to wear work clothes, so I had them on. I asked if they still needed people. They said yes, you can get on the bus. So I got on the bus, it went to Thyssen, and we were put into groups there for the different sites.

'The first day was really shitty. Nothing but dirt, dust, fumes, everything possible. As far as your health goes, it was really bad. We were cleaning up the apparatus and the machines in the smelting plant and you got dust and fumes all the time. It was so bad, people began to vomit, and one man passed out. Some collapsed on the spot, they couldn't get enough air.

'It drives you mad doing such dirty work. The boss doesn't even provide us with work shoes. Adler is someone who is entirely without pity for other human beings, he doesn't care if someone dies. It's all the same to him. The way he talks, too, about money for instance. You don't need so much at all, he says, you're single. Be glad that you've got work here!

'They don't care how you are, they don't give a shit if someone's killed. Adler's a kind of pimp. He's a clean gangster, who always manages to stay in the background. I never get the right money from him. At the moment he still owes me 800 marks.

'Some days it's such an effort, you really feel it in your back. And with the dust and fumes, it's always bad. You're always worn out, every day is bad. You can really feel it going into your lungs. I really like sport. I used to run for at least an hour every day. But now, I only need to do a couple of minutes, and I really feel it in the lungs. And the older workers, they all look terrible, the Remmert people as well. Some of them have been there three or four years and they look completely worn out. They're between 30 and 40, but they look 50, even 60. They've no hair left, they're underweight, their faces are sunken in, thin and white. I sometimes think I'm getting cancer, lung cancer, with all the stuff we're breathing in. The Oxy Plant is really terrible sometimes. I'm frightened, sometimes, of dying in pain right there, I'm frightened of that.

'Once, I had the idea that there'd been a nuclear war, that's what it looked like. All the dust and the fumes and everything – it was so bad. Like what you see in war films. In some places, there are specially dangerous jobs. In one place, for example, there's the risk from gas. It could do you in. We have to work in enclosed spaces which are terribly dangerous. There are signs warning that, if gas escapes, it would be deadly. But you wouldn't even notice that gas; you couldn't even smell it. I was often dizzy. Felt sick as well. Some days, it's difficult to stick it out. Some days I wasn't even hungry, couldn't swallow a thing, ate nothing but dust. You could really eat and swallow it, there was so much of it in the air. Lead, cadmium and all the rest, I don't even know all the things that are in it. Sometimes, I just went into a corner, vomited and sat down for a minute just to breathe.

'Even after you've showered, it settles in your lungs, it stays there. And you're working and standing in shit all day and clearing shit away. But the next day the shit's there again, it's the same thing over and over again.

'And getting so little money, I don't understand it. They want to be as rich as possible and not give a thing away, but they're already rich. If Adler gets put inside, well, Remmert keeps going and you still get fucked over. And Thyssen knows it too. Thyssen employs the people, they must know.

'What am I living for? Most of the time there's no point to my life. At first, when you're 14 or 15, slowly growing up, you've got a girlfriend, you want to sleep with her, and so what? You do it – so what? Na, it's not the best thing there is. So, if you're thinking about and wanting to achieve something, then life's got a point to it. You really want to do something and so on – but otherwise there isn't any point to it. So what's it all about?

'When was I happiest? When I was on holiday in Turkey with my parents when I was twelve. That was great. I felt quite different. And the worst? Yes, working for Adler, here at Thyssen, that's the worst there is, you'd be better off dead.'

Emergency shower

At least once a week, we're sent into the Oxy Plant, in order to get rid of the dust which constantly accumulates there. Working in enclosed spaces, at a height of 160 or 180 feet, we have to loosen the dust on the machines with compressed air, sweep it up and remove it in wheelbarrows. The dust weighs heavily on bronchial tubes and lungs. There's a lot of lead in the dust, which also contains extremely damaging metals like manganese and titanium and, of course, any amount of fine iron dust. A Thyssen foreman, who was in charge of our work, once told Yüksel, who was suffering a coughing attack and, wheezing, asked for a dust mask, 'We don't have any for you. But iron's healthy. Good for the blood. If you swallow enough iron dust you can put a magnet to your chest and it'll stay there.' Yüksel, who was not in a position to enjoy the joke, later asked our chargehand if it was true about the magnet, and was told he was a 'dumb Turk' and laughed at in front of the whole gang.

During our work, sirens and red lights constantly warn us to leave the area immediately. To underline the point, illuminated signs flash: 'When blast furnace is in operation, immediately leave the converter area!' In another place a sign read: 'Oxygen! Caution! Fire Danger!' But we still have to keep on working. A Turkish worker who got frightened and wanted to leave the danger zone was told quite bluntly by a Thyssen foreman that he had no choice but to continue working. If not, his behaviour would be seen as a refusal to work and he could go home.

A chargehand later gave us his interpretation of the frequent and regular warnings. 'Because there have been accidents in the area of the converters in the past, the steel mills are required to install this warning system. If something should go wrong again, then Thyssen aren't responsible. You were quite clearly warned not to work there.' Which means that Thyssen doesn't bear any responsibility. If something happens, then it's our own fault. The warning is quite clear, so accidents are a result of our own stupidity. But to put our minds at ease, showers have been installed at several places in this danger area. In case of fire, you can stand under them. And there are enamel EMERGENCY SHOWER signs with a pictogram, so that even immigrants who haven't mastered the language get the idea. These show the outline of a worker in full work clothes and helmet, surrounded by flames, standing under a shower.

At long last, a pleasant job near Sinter 3. We're on a roof, and are lowering pails of dust and sludge into a container by cable. The work is physically strenuous and you soon begin to sweat, but the air is bearable, and you can look across the industrial landscape and see the Rhine in the distance. What a change, for once, to be able to get out of the murky dust dungeons and into the open air. You even enjoy the rain. We enjoy the view and the absence of suffocating dust, and feel as if we've been let out of prison. After we've had almost three hours of this relative freedom we're sent to the Oxy Plant. We're taken there at full speed in the Mercedes bus, crouching on tools and wheelbarrows. On a blind corner, we almost knock down an older Turkish worker. Our ganger remarks to the Turkish driver, 'Just keep your foot down, there's a bonus for each Turk hit.' Zentel explains to us what's up. The pig-iron ferry, a gigantic piece of machinery, is stuck. Production has been completely halted. Every minute means a huge loss for the mill. Because of the blockage, a machine part has also broken, but a new one has already been brought up, and is being fitted. It's up to us to squeeze into the narrowest channels and passages to see how we can free the thing. 'Hurry up and get stuck in,' says the boss, 'you can't leave till the plant is working again. I want it sorted out by 1 pm at the latest.'

Scrambling over shaky ladders, we squeeze into cracks which are less than shoulder-width and try to knock free the layers of encrusted iron ore with crowbars, huge sledgehammers and shovels. But the crust is so hard that almost nothing comes away. Our ganger, Alfred, breaks into a rage when he sees that only small fragments are breaking off. 'You bloody niggers, you shit-wogs, fucking Turks and garlic Jews!' He includes all the nationalities known to him in one rush of abuse. 'You're all useless, you should all be put against that wall and shot in the neck!' He rages on, comes close to hitting us, and throws a pinch bar at our new Indian workmate, which fortunately only grazes his head. 'Just stay at home!' he shouts at him. 'Would I go to Turkey to pinch your job?' 'Our workmate is from India,' I try to correct him. But Alfred is certain he's right. 'I can tell a mile away if someone's from Anatolia, that's where they put the light out with a hammer!'

Alfred had also obstinately insisted to a German workmate that I come from Anatolia: 'He's always asking such dumb questions, it's unbearable.' Once he asked me why I hadn't just stayed in Turkey, and I had replied, 'Political reason, because military dictatorship there.' This led him to tell the German worker, 'Ali's working here since he can't go back to Turkey because of their crazy Khomeini.'

After an hour of goading by Alfred, the sheriff appears, and convinces himself that we won't get far with our primitive tools. Compressed air hammers and cutters are brought up, together with long scrapers. They produce the thickest possible concentrations of dust, and without masks, we have to loosen the compacted layers. Subjected to constant abuse, we crawl around inside the machine. The noise of the thundering pneumatic tools in the narrow steel passages hurts our ears. There's no protection for them. Our eyes smart and we've all got running noses; we're coughing and wheezing. It's hell. At such times, Mehmet tells me later, one would rather spend months in jail than bear this for another few hours. In such situations, one thinks up the most horrible death for Adler, and in such moments one might decide to risk everything in a smash and grab raid, or even rob a bank. Someone who's stuck here has nothing more to lose; for him, even prison has lost its terrors. Our knees are rubbed raw and bloody through our trousers and our work gloves are torn. The ferry still won't come loose. It's one, two, three o'clock. We have to go at it with our heavy equipment and swallow everything. Meanwhile, a big shot from Thyssen puts in an appearance, shouts a lot and explains that the next shift is already waiting to use the plant and we should pull our fingers out. But we're already giving everything we've got, we want nothing more than to get out of here as soon as possible. 'You'll stay in there until the plant's running again,' orders the chargehand, 'even if it takes 20 hours.'

Dr Jutta Wetzel, a specialist in internal medicine, reports on her foreign patients: 'In general, immigrant workers are employed in especially unfavourable conditions. It's not only that the jobs are notoriously dirty, but that they are often –and this is more significant – activities which must be carried out for many hours in physically constrained postures. Premature symptoms of deterioration of the spine and of the joints are the result. At the same time, conditions of intensive smoke and dust encourage the onset of bronchitic and gastric conditions. In addition, there is increased risk as a result of working with materials which damage health, for example, asbestos.

'However, I only know about such conditions from the convincing descriptions given by some patients. They were not shown to me on visits, even when I made a point of asking to see them. Despite high unemployment, companies only rarely find Germans who will do these jobs. The companies, for example steel mills, mines, road and car construction firms, shipyards and the chemical industry, are so dependent on immigrant labour that relatively high levels of sickness are tolerated. It is therefore absolutely necessary, when comparing the sickness levels of German and immigrant employees, to take into consideration their different working conditions.'

Yüksel dares to beg the Thyssen big shot for a dust mask. He's unmoved and replies, 'We don't have anything like that. Your job, for Christ's sake, is to sort things out.' At 6.15 pm, after 12 hours, this murderous shift is at last over. In the bus most of us nod off sitting uncomfortably on the tools.

Since that job, I've had chronic bronchial problems. And today, six months later, if I spit out after an attack of coughing, the saliva is often black.

Leaden limbs

Although the dust pollution in several work areas is so extreme that we don't just breathe the stuff in, but literally have to eat it, no one finds it necessary to examine either our state of health or the substances themselves. Now and then they give us some milk. That's all. I secretly collect samples of the colourful, glittering dust. A handful weighs as much as a stone. The material is sent to the independent Environmental Institute at Bremen University.

The first results of the investigation of the dust came through in late 1985. The institute has never previously detected such high concentrations of harmful substances. The analysis of the very first sample already caused the scientists difficulties, because the sensitive instruments could barely cope with such extreme concentrations. What was found reads like a Who's Who *of the world of heavy metals: astate, barium, bromine, chrome, cobalt, copper, gadolinium, iron, lead, mercury, molybdenum, niobium, palladium, rhodium, rubidium, ruthenium, selenium, strontium, technetium, titanium, vanadium, wolfram, yttrium, zinc and zircon. Lead and mercury, two metals whose levels were particularly high, present the greatest dangers. This is what the Bremen Institute has to say about them: 'Lead is a summation poison, that is, it continues to enrich itself in the body, even if only small quantities have been absorbed. This enrichment can lead to chronic lead poisoning . . . personality changes, psychic disturbances, paralysis and hereditary defects cannot be excluded.' No less horrible are the consequences of mercury which the scientists describe. 'The first symptoms of mercury poisoning appear in the sensory apparatus: tingling and loss of feeling in the hands and feet and also a numbness in the area of the mouth. Sight is affected at the same time, beginning with a narrowing of the angle of vision. Damage to the central nervous system follows, causing a decrease in muscular mobility and impaired co-ordination, resulting in serious malfunction of the equilibrium. Arms and legs often become spastic and are deformed by muscle cramps. The brain shrinks by as much as 35 per cent.'*

Even 'minimal concentrations' of either element can have toxic effects, which is why the legally allowed maximum quantities in food products are one milligram per kilo (1 ppm) for mercury and 10 milligrams per kilo (10 ppm) for lead. Our involuntary 'meal' contains 80 times more mercury (77.12 ppm) than that, and 250 times more lead (2,501 ppm).

The World Health Organization (WHO) considers a weekly intake of 3 milligrams of lead per person to be the maximum tolerable amount. Ironically, the proverbial phrase 'leaden limbs' is literally true here, since 90 per cent of the lead which enters the body finds its way into the bones.

The same is true of mercury, which also collects in the body. The actual concentration of harmful materials in the lungs, blood and bones of the steel mill workers can only be established by the analysis of blood samples. Most workers, however, constantly complained about serious problems like shortage of breath, nausea, loss of appetite, vomiting, circulation problems and also about severe bronchitis. Among scientists there are no doubts: bronchitis is closely related to ingestion of dust, and the other complaints are the classic indicators of heavy metal poisoning, especially from lead.

Once ill, forever ill

Research has been going on for decades, throughout the world, into the health risks to workers in coking plants. The principal danger comes from the coke-ovens' waste gases which contain tar-based substances. 'Tar, or tar-based substances, have a carcinogenic effect,' writes the Hamburg professor, Dr A. Manz, in the professional journal Arbeitsmedizin (Industrial Medicine). *'The only difference of opinion is over the frequency of cancer illnesses among coking plant workers. Up till now, the authorities in West Germany have recognized only skin cancer as an industrial illness caused by anthracite coal tar. In fact, the biggest problem lies elsewhere. Coking plant workers are three times more likely to suffer from lung cancer than the average German male, and are twice as likely to suffer from cancer of either the urinary tract or the main intestine. If one compares coking plant workers with office workers, the figures are even more alarming; cokery workers die ten times more frequently from cancer of the urinary tract, and get lung cancer eight times as frequently.*

The cause is well-known to scientists. Benzopyrene, a constituent of coal tar, causes cancer. Benzopyrene is also found in cigarette smoke, but in coking plants it is 300 to 400 times more concentrated. A large-scale research project on Polish coking plant workers proves that there is a close relationship between 'nonspecific, chronic illnesses of the respiratory organs (such as chronic bronchitis) and coking plant gases. But that's not all. Anyone already suffering from bronchitis is vulnerable to further illnesses because the coke gas considerably weakens the body's immunity system.'

Professor Manz makes clear what all this means: workers in coking plants have a significantly below average life expectancy.

10. THE TEST

Stop animal experiments- use Turks instead!

Grafitti on a wall in Duisburg-Wedau.

My Turkish workmate, Osman Tokar, 22, has lost his flat. Adler had constantly been late in paying his wages. His landlord, of course, wanted the rent paid on time. Osman had to move out, leaving behind his few miserable pieces of furniture. The landlord has locked them in the cellar as security, until Osman pays the 620 marks owed in rent. Since then Osman has been without a home. Sometimes he sleeps on a mattress in the hall at a cousin's, sometimes friends let him stay for a couple of days. He can't stay anywhere for longer, since everyone lives in very cramped conditions.

Osman shamefacedly admits that he has even spent the occasional night on park benches. Now, he's threatened with expulsion, because he cannot prove that he has a fixed address, and because he once applied for social security. He doesn't want to return to Turkey. He's only been there on visits, and he feels more at home in the cold foreignness of Germany than in his parents' country, where he spent only the first two years of his life. He speaks somewhat better German than Turkish, but both languages have remained foreign to him. He doesn't know where he really belongs, and feels as if someone had 'stolen his soul'.

I offer Osman my flat, but he refuses. He has already got a dry cough from the work at Thyssen, and he's afraid of sleeping 'in the prison bed beside the coke plant'. Sometimes he thinks of killing himself. Once, after I worked a whole shift with him in some dust bunker and we'd been breathing in pounds of the stuff and had both been sick during the short break, he said to me: 'Sometimes I dream about diving into the liquid fire of the blast furnace. There's a hiss, and then you don't feel anything any more.'

Embarrassed, I remain silent.

'We are only frightened because new for us and no one has done it yet,' says Osman. 'Isn't crawling like a worm in the dust and always being stamped on much worse?' He talks about a worker who accidentally fell into the blast furnace and burned up immediately. As nothing was left of him, a steel ingot was symbolically taken from the molten liquid and given to the relatives for 'burial'. In reality, his body was rolled into plates with the steel – for tanks, cars or pots.

Osman says he wants to visit an uncle in Ulm. He can live there and get work which is as unhealthy as at Thyssen, but at least there the wages are paid. At first he doesn't really come out with what it's about. 'At Thyssen we must swallow dust and work very hard. In other job we must only swallow and give our blood.' Osman says that Turks and other foreigners, like Indonesians, Latin American political refugees and Pakistanis, are much in demand for this work as *human guinea pigs* for the pharmaceutical industry. I ask him whether I can take his place for a test which is due to begin in the next few days. As compensation, I offer him half of the money for doing it: 1,000 marks. He agrees. It suits me. With my injured shoulder and the bronchitis, which is slowly becoming chronic, I should have long ago given up the heavy physical work at Thyssen.

Osman gives me the address of the LAB Institute in Neu-Ulm, a large, gloomy building with the stuffiness of a 1950's youth hostel. The hostel warden, a cheery man in his mid-20's, sits at reception. He tries to make sure that the atmosphere is relaxed. In the waiting room are a couple of punks with mohicans, who are already regulars, a couple of dark-skinned foreigners and some unemployed youths. And two down-and-outs, one smelling of spirits.

The LAB in Ulm is one of the largest private test laboratories in Europe. Its files list 2,800 test persons. There's another way of putting it. What's tested on us keeps the profits of the pharmaceutical industry healthy, and as a by-product, now and again something may turn up to help the patients.

Most human experiments don't benefit people's health; no new remedies are being researched. They're much more about marketing, market expansion, *and* advertising campaigns *for old drugs, which, under new names, are intended to open up new markets. It's quite simple: 100 drugs are on the market but all containing almost the same chemical ingredients, and now the 101st superfluous drug is to be put on the market.*

It has frequently been proved that the companies themselves tamper with and rewrite reports by reputable clinicians which are based on human tests in public hospitals. What does that say about the many private institutes which test the drugs on 'healthy' paid test-persons, and are almost completely dependent on contracts from the industry itself? One thing is certain: negative or even alarming results are always harmful to business, whether they come from doctors in the hospitals or from test 'institutes'.

Professor Eberhard Greiser, Director of the Bremen Institute for Preventive Research and Social Medicine (BIPS), say that, 'In practice, this tends to mean that tests which produce a negative result for the investigated drugs are not publicized. That is the experience which many professional experts, whom I have met over a period of time on the professional committee in the Health Ministry, have reported.'* Pharmaceutical companies give out contracts for many test series but only inform

---

* From a statement in ZDF (the second German TV channel), Reportage am Montag, 'Nebenwirkungen unbedenklich' by S. Matthies and E. Ebner, broadcast on 26 August 1985.

the Federal Health Office when results are favourable. The authorities may only learn of negative results when individual doctors or pharmaceutical company employees feel they can no longer justify these practices, and pass on the information. Officially the drug licensing and supervision offices in the Federal Republic don't even know where the studies are actually carried out. The power of the pharmaceutical companies in this country makes this possible: in other countries there are different registration requirements and regulations.

I hand over the note that Osman has given me, and ask the man at reception if there isn't some less dangerous experiment going. Osman had warned me that the scheduled test was likely to produce unpleasant side effects. 'Just don't worry,' he tries to reassure me, 'up to now everyone's come out of here alive. We're all very relaxed here.' The hostel warden adopts a very familiar conversational manner with his test persons, and explains to me, 'First of all we have to see whether you can be used at all.'

I'm sent for the required check. Several blood samples are taken, urine is sampled, then there's an electro-cardiogram and I'm measured and weighed. The final part is carried out by a doctor. At first I'm alarmed, because I take him for a fellow countryman. Fortunately he's not a Turk, but a Bulgarian exile. But he knows 'my country' well, and talks to me about Turkey.

He tells me that previously there were many more Turkish test-persons, but recently some of them have returned to Turkey. He thinks that the laboratory's experience with my countrymen has been good, they 'take a lot of punishment' and don't 'complain about every little pain'. Finally, he shines a light into my eyes, and sees that I am wearing contact lenses, but fortunately doesn't notice that they are tinted. I explain that I got them prescribed for specialized welding where glasses are a handicap.

Ali is found to be suitable, that is, he is sufficiently healthy to be given possibly harmful drugs.

Ali must sign a declaration of consent to the experiment, and is given five pages of information in German to look at which describe the drugs which are to be tested. The information is called 'Test-persons' information on the study of comparative biological responsiveness to four different compound combinations containing phenobarbitol and phenytoin'.

Ali has never heard the names of these drugs before, and even the hostel warden has difficulties pronouncing them properly. 'They're the easiest thing to forget,' he says. 'According to the information sheets, the drugs are not for an illness but rather to counter epilepsy and fever cramps in children.'

The use of such compound drugs is severely criticized by all scientists independent of the industry. The combination of two active substances prevents the adjustment of the dosage to the individual needs of the patient. Such combinations suit sloppy doctors. Furthermore, the phenobarbitol constituent belongs to the chemical family of barbiturates on which one can very quickly become dependent. In recent years, hundreds of drugs containing barbiturates have been banned because of the great risk of addiction.

So this is a drug test with well known compounds. No one explains why on earth they still need to be tested. The experiment is to extend over a period of 11 weeks, including four in-patient confinements of 24 hours each. The total fee is 2,000 marks. The information lists secondary effects which occur relatively frequently as 'tiredness, changes in mood, disturbed co-ordination, impairment of nerve functions and blood properties, effect on blood production, changes in field of vision and allergic responses with skin changes'. In 'approximately 20 per cent of the patients, inflammation of the gums appears'. If one's unlucky there may also occur 'itching skin rashes, shortage of breath, hot flushes, nausea and possibly vomiting', and 'in rare cases, serious conditions involving suffocating attacks and disturbances of blood circulation which require immediate medical attention can arise'.

But it's not so bad, because in an emergency the insurance will pay. 'If, contrary to expectation, damage to health should appear in connection with participation in this study, unlimited free medical care will be provided by the LAB or its client.' Nevertheless, 'specifically excluded is damage which is only indirectly related to participation in the study (as, for example, road accidents)'. What happens then, if a 'test-person' with 'impaired circulation and equilibrium' is involved in a traffic accident?

After signing the declaration of consent I receive a timetable for taking the drugs, and for the blood samples. I am informed that the study doesn't begin until tomorrow, but despite that I'm no longer allowed to leave the institute. 'Voluntary detention.' We're handed a blanket with a coverlet, sheets and pillowcases. The treatment rooms, the laboratory, the room for taking blood samples, and the intensive care unit, are on the first floor. The television room and the bedrooms are on the second floor.

The man sitting on the lower bunk bed doesn't look up when I come in. Two men at the table continue doing their crosswords. I go into the second bedroom which has a view of the yard. On the left, there is a car repair workshop, and in front of that, between the wall and a refuse container, some grey plastic garden furniture. On the right, there is a warehouse and wholesale business for organic products. In the background, there is a railway goods yard. A desolate district.

All those waiting to take part in the tests stress that there's absolutely no risk involved. 'The risk is much greater for them than for us,' says one. 'Because if something happened, there would be a huge scandal. And they really can't afford that.' Some are doing it for the first time. Some are 'professional' test-persons, many of them foreigners, who go from institute to institute, and sometimes expose themselves to dangerous double tests. It's called 'pharma-prostitution' in the trade. There are recruiters and touts who sign up losers of all sorts to be used as guinea pigs.

At suppertime, everyone meets. Four women sit together. On reception, they have to undergo a pregnancy test. If, however, they should become pregnant during the drug tests, which usually last for months, serious and permanent damage can occur to their babies. In this eventuality, the LAB promises 'medical and spiritual aid' – whatever that might be.

Everyone gets their plate packed through a hatch: bread, butter, a couple of slices of cheese, a tomato, a cucumber, a pepper. *Bonnie and Clyde* is on in the TV room. The curtains are drawn to shield the television from the evening sun. The aerial is broken. One person has to hold it, so that the film is faintly visible. The room smells of cigarette ash and stale smoke. Hardly anyone can sleep and the television programmes are over. We sit silently in the yard till after midnight, smoking and drinking flat water from paper cups: water is the only thing we're still allowed.

People lying in the beds stare at the ceiling or try to sleep. Someone has fallen asleep next to his transistor radio, 'Music after Midnight' at full volume. No one puts the light off. From 2.30 am, 'Music till Early Morning'. Then I switch the radio off and put out the harsh neon light. From the goods yard, there's the sound of wagons being shunted together. The wind blows the empty plastic cups across the yard. Someone masturbates under the blanket, on and on, without finding release.

At 6 o'clock the door opens. 'Time to get up!' Silently, without greetings, we get up. Everyone is preoccupied with themselves. My urine bottle has the number 4. That means at 6.04 am a catheter in the arm, at 7.04 am an intake of drugs, at 8.04 am a blood sample, and so on.

The first few times we still queue up. Later we get to know who's in front and who's behind, and know when it's our turn. The man behind me has just been released from prison and couldn't find work anywhere. No one asks him any questions here. The two young guys who stab the catheters into the crook of our arms chat about their next exams. They haven't completed their medical studies yet. The two of them supervise the intake of drugs. While they watch, I have to swallow the two capsules. First of all, I notice how my field of vision is growing smaller. I try to look into the yard, but the sun is too strong and hurts my eyes. I lie on the bed and doze. I get up like a sleepwalker for the hourly blood withdrawals. Everyone looks pale and haggard. More and more people don't report for their medication and have to be fetched from their beds. A woman complains of heat convulsions, attacks of dizziness and circulatory problems. Her arm feels cold, furred and numb.

I feel awful the next day. It's a pointless experiment, because all the effects are well known. We are just experiencing them: considerable giddiness, bad headaches, loss of balance, a dulling of the senses, and, in addition, we repeatedly doze off. Our gums are bleeding badly. Blood samples have been taken seven times but we still have to be constantly available. The others also have serious complaints.

Only when one person actually mentions it, does it turn out that almost every one of us has a headache. Apparently, they all said nothing out of fear of not being allowed to take part in another experiment. One test-human, aged 39 and unemployed for three years, tells me, 'I've experienced far worse experiments in the intensive care section, connected up to tubes. Most of our group had to give up and some had to be carried to bed afterwards.' He tells me of a Munich institute where especially dangerous experiments are carried out 'far beyond the pain threshold. They're always looking for people.' Another talks about a 'psychobunker' near Munich, where experiments take place in total darkness, often lasting as long as four weeks. There's a heart centre in Munich, says an 18-year-old, where you can take part in dangerous experiments and 'let your heart be played around with for a bit of money'.

After the 'first course', that is, after 24 hours, I decide to break off the experiment. Had I continued, I would have been confined on another three occasions during the next 11 weeks. And the secondary effects get worse, not better. On top of that, one would have had to turn up daily at seven o'clock throughout the 11 weeks, including Saturday and Sunday, for the blood-sampling, and also collect all one's urine during the 11 weeks in plastic containers. Anyone abandoning the test before the end doesn't get a penny.

Professor Riedlbrock of Frankfurt believes that 'perhaps two thirds of these biological response studies are unnecessary'. These are studies which are adapted for commercial purposes, and in which there is no longer a proper relationship between benefit and expenditure.'* There have already been deaths during such tests. Two years ago, for example, the 30-year old Irish professional test person, Neill Rush, collapsed and died during a test series. The company was testing a drug to counter heart rythm disturbance. The day before, in a different laboratory, Rush had allowed Deporil, a psycho-pharmacological drug, to be tested on him. According to the autopsy, the cause of sudden death was the mixing of the two drugs. A minimum demand would be to require the pharmaceutical industry to issue test-person licenses in order to prevent such 'double experiments'.

One of the test-persons at the LAB has given me another address, BIO-DESIGN, in Freiburg im Breisgau. 'They always need people and pay well. And the food's a lot better than it is here.' So I travel there next. In contrast to the LAB, which was somewhat down at heel, BIO-DESIGN is a shiny new futuristic laboratory, a bit like a space station. The lady at reception

---

* Statement in ZDF (the second German TV channel), Reportage am Montag, 'Nebenwirkungen unbedenklich' by S. Matthies and E. Ebner, broadcast on 26 August 1985.

immediately puts the same precautionary question as Adler does when someone new applies, only more politely. 'Who referred you to us?' I give the name of the contact from the LAB.

They immediately have a tempting offer for Ali, 2,500 marks for 15 days, but 'completely in-house'. They respond to his question, 'And must pay tax?' with 'No, it's not registered here. This is a health service.' They still seem to be short of brave test-persons for the experiment, because they try to tempt me with an advance. 'If you should decide to take part, we could, as an exception, consider an advance. You will also be well looked after here. The food is free.' I ask, 'And what is for so much money? What is done?' A younger laboratory employee, with a melancholy smile, explains the test. 'It's an Aldosteron antagonist, the substance is called Mesperinon. It has the effect of flushing abnormal water accumulation through the kidneys. It also affects the hormonal balance. The drugs already on the market belong to the Spironolacton family. It's been established that with this substance, if taken over a longer period, so-called feminization results; that is, the formation of breasts in men. However, in a two week test, this is not likely to occur.'

Ali: 'It is safe?'

Laboratory employee: 'Probably. Of course, that's the point of the experiment. One can never be certain.'

Ali: 'And if happens, goes away again?'

Laboratory employee (reassuring): 'Yes, of course, it regresses again.'

Here, I am quite clearly being wrongly informed. The development of breasts in men has to be removed by an operation. That, at any rate, is the unanimous medical opinion. The employee also fails to tell the truth on another point. To Ali's question, 'What happen to potency? Stay?' the reply is, 'Oh, in that respect, no change is expected.' In fact, there is virtually no research experience available on the effects of Mesperinon on humans. The information sheet accompanying the experiment emphasizes that secondary effects like, 'head-aches, dizziness, absent-mindedness, stomach pains, skin changes' can be expected, and with higher dosages 'formation of breasts and impotence' are likely. The contract contains the threat that 'if a test is broken off without notice, then BIO-DESIGN can demand compensation from the test-person for that part of the expenditure which has already been used in carrying out the test . . .' BIO-DESIGN doesn't seem to be much bothered by the immorality of this contract. It puts the test-persons under incredible pressure to hold out at all costs, despite all the possible pain and side effects.

Fortunately, I am not dependent on the temptingly large sums of money and can afford to decline the offer with thanks. Many can't do that. Companies like LAB and BIO-DESIGN profit from the economic crisis, which drives more and more people to them.

Those responsible, stonewall at so-called 'Ethics Commis-sions' on which scientists and even clergymen sit. Ethics Commissions are voluntary control committees whose votes are legally binding only in the US and Japan, but not in West Germany.

Ethics is a cynical term in this context. These commissions can be replaced by the company bosses at any time or dropped altogether. And even if official bodies were involved, as is the case in other countries, their competence extends only to *medical* questions. A *human* ethic, however, would demand, at the very least, that one also takes into account the despair of people who have been forced to the margins of society, and who are then prepared to entertain suicide by instalments.

My suggestion is that a law should be passed which requires the top earners in the pharmaceutical industry to make them-selves available for tests. The advantages would be immense. Physically, these people are mostly in a far better state than many of the worn-out professional test-persons and because of their incomes they could afford much longer holidays and rest cures. The number of experiments would decline drastically and be restricted to a useful minimum. The proposal is quite serious. Sixty years ago, drug researchers still tested new discoveries on themselves.

I found out for myself just how frequently the 'rare' side effects appear. After returning from my journey through the pharmaceutical laboratories, the gums on my lower jaw began to swell and suppurate. The dentist diagnosed gum ulceration and he immediately suspected the correct reason. 'Are you taking drugs which contain Phenytoin?' He had no hesitation in ascribing my 'rare' symptoms to this drug.

11. PROMOTION

I feel worn out and ill and unable to continue working at Thyssen, even though I know plenty of workers who, despite illness and injuries, will go on slaving for Adler; who, in spite of 'flu and fever, keep on going for 16 hours at a stretch, afraid that otherwise someone else will be hired in their place. At work, a piece of iron falls on Mehmet's foot. Because he had no work shoes with reinforced toecaps, his foot swells up so much that he has to cut open the side of his shoe and tie wire round it to hold it together. He limps to work, in great pain, his teeth clenched together, and doesn't utter a word of complaint.

I think now I can afford to take a gamble and make a virtue out of necessity; I've heard that Adler is having problems with his trusty and chauffeur so I decide to try and get the driver's job by means of a trick. I make an appointment with Adler about wages owed. As usual, he's bad-tempered and asks why I have been absent from work for several days. When I apologize and tell him that I can guarantee my complete recovery and that it won't happen again, he relents and says I should come again the following day. 'But punctually, if you please, two o'clock on the dot.' The same old story. Who doesn't show up the next day? Adler. Three hours later, at almost five o'clock, I manage to catch up with him at his house. He's unfriendly right from the start. 'Nothing can be done now. You should have come earlier. I'm sitting in the bath now.' In fact, he's fully dressed.

Ali: 'Can still wait and sit on steps. Have already waited three hours.'

Adler (angry): 'No. You can't do that. Come back tomorrow.'

Ali: 'Don't want money now, just ask question . . .'

Adler: 'No, can't be done. Ring tomorrow.'

Ali: 'Please, only five minutes. Travelled one hour to get here.'

Adler: 'Ring me tomorrow. We can talk about it on the phone. I can't do anything about it.'

Ali: 'I have important matter. I must help you.'

Adler (curious, alarmed): 'Well, what?'

Ali: 'I must help, otherwise something will happen to you.'

Adler: 'Me? Why? Who?'

Ali: 'I come again, if you are in the bath.'

Adler: 'No, wait, come in.'

Hesitatingly, I follow him into his office, and reveal that one of the workers, whom Adler still owes money, wants to teach him a lesson, but that Ali won't allow it. In what follows, I play the part of someone, awkwardly over-zealous, who is willing even to lay down his life for his master. 'I can do karate, special Turkish karate, called Sisu.' It's all complete nonsense, of course, I don't know any karate, and 'Sisu' is a Finnish word meaning endurance, patience, perseverance. 'If someone wants to harm you, I help you. One blow and he's gone.' To emphasize my fierce determination I bring my fist down on Adler's desk with as much force as I can muster. Adler looks me up and down, half impressed, half irritated. 'But who wants to touch me?' he asks. 'It's good and quite right that you should defend me, but which dirty rat wants to harm me?' 'I don't know name now,' I say, 'but I tell him, who wants to kill Adler, has to kill Ali. I am Adler's man.'

Adler has swallowed the bait. For five minutes, he reads out the names of past and present Turkish and Arab employees, to whom he clearly still owes money and who, in his eyes, have now all become potential murderers. I ask him to repeat one or two but then, each time, I firmly shake my head, the avenger's name is not there. In order not to actually bring any colleague under suspicion, I invent a phantom-avenger, an 'Arab, who's member of a Turkish gang', with huge fists – I demonstrate – who has recently 'with one blow smashed half of face' of a German who had 'offended and cheated' him. 'Nose broken, eye shut, whole face kaput.' Adler looks worried, so I mention my other assets: that I not only 'can do karate, but was for long time taxi driver' and had previously been 'chauffeur of another boss with big factory'. 'What kind of factory?' Adler asks, assuming a professional manner. 'Make talking machines,' I explain. 'You mean walkie-talkies,' Adler corrects me. (If need be, I could even get a reference from the company, because the firm's boss is a friend of mine.) 'I still have uniform in cupboard,' I boast, 'with nice hat, good material.'

'Ah yes, interesting,' says Adler, 'are you a good driver, then?' 'Sure, no problem,' I reply, 'boss could always sleep when I drive, and I repair everything when auto kaput.' A complete lie again, but I can probably rely on Adler's almost-new Mercedes 280 SE, equipped with every possible extra. 'Yeah, we can talk about that,' says Adler. 'I always need to get around, and you can keep troublesome guys away from me as well. You just tell me the names. I've got a direct line to the aliens' department. They'll be kicked out before they know what's hit them.' 'Just let me do,' I try to deflect him. 'You need have no more fear, when they know I am Adler's man, one blow from Ali and they're dead, one blow and they're gone. No police needed, I do better.' 'Well, good,' says Adler. 'Come back on Monday at 10.30 and we'll give it a go.'

And so it was that Ali was promoted from swallower of dust and labourer to chauffeur and bodyguard. It seems there are still quite undreamt of opportunities for advancement in our society, even for the lowliest guest worker.

Adler immediately tries to introduce his job creation measure, as is his way, with a new fraud. 'You're still sick aren't you?' he says. 'Look, we'll register you with the health insurance right away. You go to the doctor, get a note, then I don't need to pay you any money, the insurance will pay, and you'll already be driving for me.'

It was to be a difficult task of self-denial, ferrying Adler around during the following weeks. He found fault at every touch of the steering wheel. 'Take the driving seriously, if you please! . . . And that's the last risk you take! . . . How often do I have to tell you, these are valuable goods you're driving around. The car costs a lot of money! . . . I want to be driven sensibly and safely. You're responsible for getting me and the car home all in one piece.' In fact, I already drive slowly and carefully. It can hardly be called driving at all, more a sort of gentle gliding. However, Adler has exaggerated fears. Perhaps he needs this endless fault-finding as a kind of self-justification.

Usually, Adler summons Ali to his house 20 to 50 minutes early. That's when Ali feels himself misused as an 'alarm call'. Ali rings. It's a while before Adler calls down in a sleepy voice, 'Wait outside. It'll be ten minutes.'

Then I wait and wait. If it's raining, there's nowhere to shelter. It doesn't occur to Adler to throw down the key so that Ali can sit in the Mercedes.

The expensive suburb wakes up at about eight or nine o'clock. Shutters are raised, windows are slowly opened. Garage doors slide up automatically and affluent owners drive off to offices in their sleek limousines. A wife hangs a magnificent cage with exotic birds at the window. The front gardens are very carefully tended, and the lawns are always trimmed. Occasionally, Ali is summoned to Adler as early as 7 or 8 am , for departure half an hour or an hour later. As a rule, however, Adler's day doesn't begin before ten or eleven o'clock, and it's often already over by two or three, or, exceptionally, four. In between, there's often an hour's lunchbreak. Frequently, the day's work for Adler consists solely of visiting various banks in Oberhausen and Dinslaken and checking the payments made into his accounts. Strangely enough, all the banks are well outside the district in which he lives. Then there's also usually a visit to his friend and business partner, Remmert, almost always at a time when workers aren't coming off shifts, so that he avoids 'impertinent questions' and 'outrageous wage demands'. On the way back, a stop is often made at his indoor tennis club and restaurant, just to 'make sure everything's all right', or perhaps he'll meet his 'tax defrauder', a tax consultant who is a close friend. Officially, Adler puts his annual turnover at 'between 500,000 and 1 million' marks and he has hardly any overheads. In fact, given his business behaviour, the real turnover is likely to be many times that. The money from Thyssen and for his other unregistered illegal workers alone, adds up to more.

It's torture driving him around. He's constantly finding fault, constantly sees his life in danger. I often have the impression that I don't have a real person of flesh and blood behind me, but an extremely fragile, parchment mummy, in a delicate glass container, afraid of falling apart at the least touch of the brakes. He's constantly correcting me, or even shouting at me. 'Don't overtake! Drive slowly, you fool!' Or he employs one of his catch phrases, 'Please take the job seriously,' or 'We must always remain respectable. We are not hooligans.' All this at a speed of under 30 mph in towns and less than 85 on the motorway. He's not worried about the road safety of others, he has an abstract fear for his own valuable and precious life. He also has a real phobia about the police. If he becomes aware of a policeman or a patrol car, he has me take the nearest turn-off or make a great detour in order to be out of sight as fast as possible.

He never looks back. It's his motto. True to his favourite 1960's hit, 'One hundred men and only one order'* he leaves only

---

* 'Hundert Mann und ein Befehl', a hit for the German singer Freddy Quinn. (Trans.)

'scorched earth' behind him: 'A hundred men and only one order/And a road that no one wants to take/Day in, day out who knows where to/Burnt earth and what's the sense of it?'

Once, I'm almost found out. Adler notices me giving a hand signal to the photographer on the other side of the street, who had almost missed our departure. 'To whom did you wave?' he asks, extremely suspicious. 'Not wave,' I throw him off the scent, 'was only quick reflex move for karate training. When sit long time, must always test reactions, test speed of arm, leg, hand.' And as corroboration I make swift, jabbing movements with arms and hands while I'm driving, which he at first regards with some astonishment. To further underline my diligence in training (and also to make him keep his distance should my cover ever be blown) I tell him that my lightning-fast responses are much feared at the karate club. Another member who had rashly got in the way of a blow, had spent 'four days in a coma'. My claim that I could break bricks in half 'two together, but old stones, not new', with the edge of my hand, had already impressed him. 'One blow from Ali can kill,' I execute a hand movement in his direction. However, in order not to alarm him any further, I add, 'But we only do when attack us, and never start fight.' If he only knew that I reject fighting and the use of weapons on principle, and that my only strength in tricky situations is to run away!

'Stop jumping around in my car, if you please, you'll tear the whole seat loose. You can do that when you're outside,' he suddenly shouts for no reason. For the seats are so solid that my harmless movements could hardly damage them.

I want to stress the seriousness of my karate-training and thereby completely dispel his initial suspicions. So when I have to spend a long time waiting for him outside Ruhr Coal Heating Technology in Essen, I carry out shadow fighting and boxing movements in front of his car. I cause an uproar among the secretaries of the Medical Insurance Association on the other side of the road, who come to the windows of the multistorey office block to wave and to egg this wild bodyguard on. I wave back, and manage to disrupt work at Medical Insurance for at least a quarter of an hour. When Adler comes back to find Ali leaping around and crowds at the windows, he's angry. 'Stop that at once, you idiot, people will start talking about me. You can do that in your monkey house in Diesel Street, or in your Turkish club.' Ali replies, 'Understood. But you say, can do outside.' Ali flings open the car door for his boss and then lets himself in with his usual obsequious manner.

Sometimes, I hear my boss talking about firing 'difficult' and 'tiresome' people. His voice isn't in the least irritable or angry, as one might expect, but instead takes on a satisfied expression. 'Hello, my dear, listen,' he says, and his voice over the car phone is sugary. 'I'm rid of another pain in the arse. I've just been to Ruhr Coal. T. will be sacked tomorrow. Yes, isn't it fantastic!' Or, again on the car phone, while he's inviting friends from industry and politics, including a West German MP, for a weekend trip to Holland on his motor yacht, he reports to one of his business friends, 'One less bit of baggage. Sacked today. Bang, over and done with. He had really annoyed me.' On another occasion, he philosophizes over the phone. 'Sometimes you just have to hit hard. Never mind the tears. The worst mistake is to be soft, then you might as well pack up and go home!'

He can afford to fire 'people' according to his mood and whims. Increasing unemployment drives more and more desperate people into his arms, ready for work under almost any conditions. He often doesn't even know the people he exploits, he just collects the money. He also says over the car phone, 'Ruhr Coal comes to me [they've installed some new plant] and tells me, listen, we can't take anyone on, complete ban on recruitment, but we need electricians. So we went away, past Cologne, made a deal with the employment office there, started off some electricians. The money just flowed into my account, I never saw the people, only the money.' [Laughs.] 'You've got to be on the ball. You always think of something when you have to.' And another time he says, 'I really prefer the big ones. I've got contacts all over Steag. We've worked in all the power stations. Thyssen, Ruhr Coal, Ruhr Chemicals, General Electric in Holland, all companies with an international reputation. No official, no factory inspector's office, dares go near them. What we do or don't do is up to us. The men knock up the hours till they drop. The main thing is that we carry out the job quickly and discreetly. The less men there are, the better they like it, because it's more inconspicuous. I only need half the people, and the money's still right.'

On occasion, he enviously admits that some of his competitors can teach him a few tricks. Some manage to 'make money twice over' with the poisonous sludge they've been contracted to 'remove'. 'F. had a contract with Ruhr Coal to get rid of Emscher River sludge. Makes a mint doing that. And makes a mint with it a second time. Puts it through a coal grinder and sells it for heating. There's only one problem, you can't store coal dust in a silo. It generates gases and fumes which can explode at any moment. Same thing with the coal tip here in Oberhausen. The city gave it to a Dutchman. The Dutchman gets his money for each cubic metre he removes from the tip. What does the guy do with it? He grinds the stuff down and sells it to tennis clubs. Tennis courts, that's the business right now. There's acid in it and all kinds of poison. So there are ugly wounds if someone falls over on that. That's what you've got to be able to do: make money out of shit, and be paid for it on top of that. Boy, oh boy, some people just stick their finger in shit, and when they pull it out, there's gold on it!'

Adler may have built his fortune on dirt and dust or, to use his own language, on shit, but where his own person is concerned, he observes the most fastidious cleanliness and neatness. He has an almost hysterical fear of contact with the messy side of life. To him, his slave workers are an unclean caste, untouchables. They disgust him and he would like to keep as much distance from them as possible. When they surprise him at home with their wage demands, his indignation is not only due to the threatened financial loss, but also to his horror at the direct confrontation with, and closeness to, sweat, filth and misery, even though the workers always call on him cleanly and respectably dressed. I was always the only exception. I quite deliberately appeared in his clean suburb wearing my dirty, oil-smeared work clothes, my face blackened by soot and dust.

Since then, Ali's clothes have adjusted to Adler's Mercedes. Pressed trousers, freshly laundered white or grey shirt, tie, and no heavy, mucky boots, but polished leather slip-ons. Nevertheless, for Adler, Ali still counts as part of the proletarian underworld. His address in Diesel Street is a stigma. In Adler's eyes, it's where the lowest of the low live in the shit, and go to work in the shit next door.

One day, when Ali once again has to wait in front of Adler's house at half past seven in the morning, he feels the urgent need to go to the toilet. He rings the bell and asks Adler if he can use his toilet.

Adler: 'Do you need big or small?'

Ali: 'Everything.'

Adler (disgusted): 'Well, just do it outside.'

Ali: 'Where shall I outside?'

Adler: 'Do it round the corner, somewhere, go on.'

Ali: 'Where in the corner?'

Adler: 'Eh, what the fuck does it matter.'

He sends Ali into the street like a dog. Anyway there's no possibility of shitting in his front garden, it's open on all sides. I long to lay a turd on the bonnet of his Mercedes, right on the star. Ten minutes later, when Adler comes down, I ask him, 'Your toilet is broken?'

Adler: 'No, it's not broken. It's just we don't really allow it to be used. You know, with strangers and so on, I'll tell you quite straight, because we're worried about disease. There are so many things going round. You never know where you're going to pick up an infection. You understand? And in that area, after all, the risk of infection is fairly large.'

Ali: 'When guests come they always go outside?'

Adler (embarrassed, hesitates): 'I have, as I already said, no guests, but my workmen and so on don't sit on my toilet, they all know that. They don't bother asking. So I am, with regard to that, very, very careful.'

Ali: 'You are frightened of Aitchs?'

Adler: 'You mean Aids, yeah? Everyone is frightened, aren't they, but I . . . take precautions. For example, I never go when I'm somewhere else, to strange toilets or anything. I just don't.'

Ali: 'Hm.'

Adler: 'I don't. I always try to work it so that I can do the business at home and not use any strange toilets.'

Ali: 'Hmm.'

Adler: 'Not the public ones, or any others, when I'm visiting . . . I hardly ever shake anyone's hand or anything like that. And if I have to shake hands with someone, then I try and wash immediately afterwards.'

Ali: 'If all people think like you, then nothing would happen?'

Adler: 'No more disease would occur, that's right. But everyone doesn't think like that. Some people are real pigs. You feel really sick, if you think about it.'

If ever Adler is charged with his crimes, then someone should take him to the Remmert toilets. For the workers there are only two: both covered in filth. The company doesn't provide toilet paper and the toilets are virtually never cleaned. One lavatory has no door. Since there's always a queue, one just squats on it anyway. A German has written on the door in felt tip, 'wogs only'.

Sometimes, on the motorway between Oberhausen and

Essen, or driving towards Wesel, when the landscape is gliding past, and no telephone calls have to be made, Adler starts to philosophize. Then he turns down German-language Radio Luxemburg, his favourite radio station, which soothes him with its all's-well-with-the-world programmes. Normally taciturn and uninformative towards his Turkish driver, on these occasions Adler, the prospering businessman, suddenly feels the need to articulate his profound thoughts on the state of the nation, and share them with me.

'Good morning, Germany, I love you . . .' is coming from the radio as I ask him, 'Mr Adler, how long you own boss and business man?' 'For five years,' Adler says, and explains that before that he was chief buyer for the MAN Gutehoffnung steel mill. 'But in those five years I learned more than in the whole of the rest of my life. And more about villains and so on.'

Ali: 'But earned money like never before? What kind of villain?'

Adler: 'Yeah, earning money is part of it. But here in Germany there's a whole lot of gangsters, who are too lazy to work and are always trying to get their hands on your wallet. They only want to shit on you. And our own people, our own workers, are no longer what the German worker once was in terms of hard work and skill. Of course Hitler was a dictator, but in tht respect . . .'

Ali: 'But killed people.'

Adler: 'Yes, and he also started wars that weren't really necessary.'

Ali: 'Because he lost them?'

Adler: 'Yes, because he expanded too fast and still wanted to get bigger and bigger. Above all, one can disagree with what he did to the Jews. But they're not much liked anywhere, the Jews . . . What's easily forgotten today is that he gave everyone bread and work. When he was in power, there were no unemployed . . . If we have another one, two million unemployed, then we'll get something like Hitler again. You can rely on that. Then there'll be real trouble here, with riots and everything.'

Ali: 'Yes, then is our turn. Then, we are the Jews.'

Adler (laughs): 'Don't worry about it, we won't gas you right away. I don't think so. We need you to work. With the Jews, that goes back thousands of years. You see, the Jews were always merchants and always had other people working for them. And the things that other people sweated over, they bought up cheap and sold dear. That's the Jews. The Jews are born idle, and don't want to work and have always got rich at the expense of other people, that's why no one likes them, whether in Germany or in America or in Russia or Poland. The Turks, that's something else again. You know yourself that your people can get stuck into things. Laws would be made that all of them would have to leave within a year. If, for example, there were another million unemployed.'

Ali: 'You think, will be more?'

Adler: 'Yeah, everyone who knows anything about it says so. The politicians and the top people in industry. Only you can't say it to the people in the street. There are more and more computers and robots, for example. If I could substitute machines for the people I've got – if each machine cost, say 100,000 marks – if that meant three men less, then I would do it. With a machine I don't get any aggravation.'

Ali: 'Mhm.'

Adler: 'Do you understand? It's more reliable. The machine works more smoothly. That's how it is, it's the same everywhere, look at the big factories, everything's automated. The jobs like steel construction and pipe-laying, countries like Nigeria or East Germany can do that much cheaper than we can, because our wage costs are far too high. We're not competitive any more. Everyone's always talking about reducing unemployment, only no one manages to do it. In our economic system, it's no longer possible, on the contrary. The young kids who are coming out of school, they want jobs, but there aren't any. It's all nonsense – early retirement, you can forget it. It's like in Ancient Egypt. People used to say, first there are seven fat years, and then seven lean years. That's what's happening now, we've had 40 fat years and now we've got to adjust to the lean years, till maybe eventually there's a new military conflict or something, so that things need to be rebuilt again.'

Ali: 'You think war comes again?'

Adler: 'Yeah, if there's even more unemployed, there'll be civil war in Germany, anyway. It's quite possible. If there's another million unemployed, they'll take to the streets, they'll go on the barricades. There'll be chaos. Law and order will be finished.'

Meanwhile, there's a report on the car radio: 'Residence permits of foreigners are to be shortened or rescinded if marriage to a German has failed . . .'

Adler: 'There you are!'

Radio: '. . . rejected the case brought by a Turkish man who had been living in Germany for five years. His German wife had applied for a divorce, and had already been awarded custody of a common child. As a consequence, the city of Kassel limited the man's permit of residence till the end of August this year.'

Adler: 'You see, it's happening everywhere!'

Ali: 'But what do you think of it? They marry, but woman now maybe has other man and off, out, send away. Cannot see own child any more!'

Adler (unmoved): 'Has to go back, no question about it. You heard it. In any case, it was a political mistake. When we had the economic miracle, we opened the floodgates far too wide and all the Turks who wanted to come, could come, and all the Italians who wanted to come, could come . . . Politically, that was a big mistake, and they shouldn't have done it.'

Ali: 'But we not just come by ourselves, were brought, and then no computer, need people.'

Adler: 'Yes, but it was a double-edged sword. They regret it today. The Turks came, and all the heavy, dirty work was done by the foreigners, but the German didn't work any more, he didn't want to get his hands dirty any more. And that mentality's still there. The German doesn't want to work any more and causes a lot more problems.

'It was a fundamental mistake to let in so many foreigners. But I'm also convinced that if all the Turks were gone – we've got 2.3 million unemployed now – then we'd only have a fraction less unemployed. It's nothing to do with the Turks . . . If all the Turks were gone now, we would have maybe 100,000 less unemployed, but what difference is that going to make?'

Our conversation is interrupted by another news report: '. . . he is accused of . . . Veba, Klöckner, Krupp, Mannesmann and eleven others . . . he facilitated payment of these donations, by . . .'

Ali: 'This . . . economics minister, he will go to jail?'*

Adler: 'No, absolutely impossible, half the government would have to go to jail in that case. It can't happen.'

Ali: 'Make millions profit, and still want more.'

Adler: 'Well, of course, you always want more money. It's human nature, isn't it?'

Ali's interim testimonial from Adler after his promotion
Testimonial

Mr Ali Levent Si   of 10 Dieselstr., 41 Duisburg is employed by us.
Through his outstanding work, punctuality and diligence on various building sites he has proved himself so valuable that we have recently made him our head chauffeur.

His work involves attendance and care of the vehicle as well as driving of our Mercedes 280 E.

We are very pleased with Mr Si   .
We intend at a later date to place him in charge.

---

* A reference to the former economics minister, Count Lambsdorff, of the Free Democratic Party, accused of accepting illegal payments from private companies, largely for party funds. He was subsequently acquitted. (Trans.)

12. THE WORKS MEETING

A 'works meeting', Adler call it, when he orders his 'people' to a back room in the Sportlereck pub in Skagerrak Street, ten minutes' walk from Remmert's company yard. While I'm driving him there, he talks over the car phone to one of his confidants. He talks about having to make sure that there's 'peace and quiet', that 'everyone's in line', and that he would prefer to have a regular nucleus working legally for a while, rather than be 'up to your neck in the shit' afterwards. The talk with his men is fixed for 4 pm. Attendance is obligatory – after working hours and, of course, unpaid.

Ali has to carry Adler's briefcase for him. 'You just stick close to me now,' he says to me. 'If someone comes too close, you stick in and don't pull any punches.' 'Is clear,' I reassure him. I have a sinking feeling in my stomach because I now have to appear in front of my former workmates and friends as an arselicker and as Adler's bodyguard.

The men are already sitting round a large table, new faces among them. Adler sits himself down at the head of the table, and motions to me to squeeze in beside him. I wink at some mates. I doubt whether they understand me. 'Quiet now!' Adler ends their conversations, adding, quite incomprehensibly for most of them, 'This isn't a Jew school, you know.' The room is quiet. Everyone looks expectantly at Adler, waiting for what he's going to reveal to them. His speech begins in quite an unaccustomed manner: 'My dear fellow workers . . .' Kemal kicks me under the table, he can't suppress a laugh. 'I've brought you all here, because we really must at last bring this team up to scratch now. It's been claimed that people are working black for us, and the name of Remmert has even been mentioned on the radio in this context. This sort of thing is, of course, bad for business, and I warn everyone against spreading these rumours. The way things look now, we want to provide a nucleus of employees with fixed job contracts. We would like to make use of a device which the government has made available to us, to sign six-month contracts with reliable people so as to see who's working well for us and who's not so good. One can't look inside people's heads, after all. If we click as a team then we can talk about things again. There are several companies at Thyssen who are not operating on as legal a basis as we now are.'

He explains that 'three thousand hours a month are certain' from Thyssen at the moment, as well as special jobs on top of that, and he hopes that will continue 'year in year out, assuming that the economic climate continues to be as favourable as it is now and Thyssen doesn't suddenly call it all off'.

He has Ali fetch the waitress and declares grandly, 'Right, *one* drink for everyone now, lemonade, cola or beer; this round's on me!' Then he clarifies matters for the sceptical 'dear fellow workers' sitting in front of him. 'Everybody, listen! I'm now going to tell you what the rates are.' He talks about his rates as if they were official and binding and the result of negotiations with the trade unions. 'The rates are as follows, to make sure there are no misunderstandings: people from 18 to 21, 8.50 marks. People who are bachelors and over 21, 9 marks. People who are married, 10 marks.' (Very few of us are married.) 'I've graded it a little,' he justifies himself, 'because a married man, that's obvious, has more expenses. I've graduated this wage rate with social considerations in mind, if you like.' Adler looks sternly round the table. 'If someone doesn't agree with it, he should stand up and leave!'

No one moves. No one dares to say what he thinks. For most, it's not a question of earning a living, it's just a question of survival. Each one knows that there are dozens of others on the street who would be ready to take his place without hesitation.

'Are the 8 marks 50, net?' ventures Nedim.

Adler (short): 'We only pay wages gross.'

Nedim: 'But that only leaves 5 or 6 marks clear.'

Adler: 'I don't have the tables for unmarried men in my head right now. Could be. But once and for all: we only pay gross. We don't only pay for work done, but also according to social circumstances. The cake that has to be divided up is only so large, and so one has to take account of the social aspects.'

Colleagues tell me that the Thyssen cake alone is worth 52 marks per worker per hour. That is supposed to include dust, dirt, heat and other bonuses for health risks, to say nothing of overtime bonuses. For Thyssen, this per capita money for people from Adler is still cheaper than employing full-time workers themselves. Paid holidays, Christmas bonus, continued payment of wages during illness, all the other usual social benefits, including protection against unfair dismissal, disappear. Of the the 52 marks, Adler gives Remmert 27. If one makes the generous assumption that this time – unusually for him – he doesn't stick the insurance contributions straight into his own pocket, and passes on 9 marks, then that leaves him 16 marks per hour. Multiplied 3,000 times a month, that makes 48,000 marks a month that Adler gets from Thyssen alone.

'So, let's take down the names of the individual workers!' When he looks at the depressed and despairing faces around him, he produces one of the comforting phrases from his repertoire. 'I know that's not very much at the moment. But I'm quite prepared, as I said we haven't known one another very long, once we get to know one another better, in six months' time, then you can talk to me about wage rises, and I'm certain it'll be possible to do something.' Everyone who knows him, knows that these are empty promises.

'Right, and something else,' Adler raises his hand, 'in future there will be no more absences from work. We're running a clean shop from now on, and aren't taking anyone else on. In future, if anyone doesn't turn up, then we'll have to do without him. Someone else will have to take his place. That should be quite clear. I'm not going to have any crap!'

He looks sharply at 23-year-old Mustafa. 'That goes for you too. You didn't turn up the day before yesterday. That's the last time.' Mustafa apologizes, saying that he had to take his wife to hospital, because she had given birth to a son. Instead of congratulating him, Adler pretends he hasn't heard, and repeats, 'But that was the very last time.' Although no sick pay has ever been paid and we frequently turn up for work only to be sent back home again, he disposes of our time and our lives as if we were serfs. He's just as rude to the German, Walter Recht. 'Your endless absences from work have got to stop now, once and for all, as well. Otherwise . . .'

Walter (dejectedly): 'Mr Adler, we had worked 20 hours from Saturday to Sunday. I only got home at quarter to three and at half past I had to call an ambulance for my wife, who had to have an operation in hospital immediately. But I told Mr Flachmann right away.' Adler doesn't listen, and makes himself clear. 'If you don't take note of what I'm saying, I'll do what I used to do. If someone said they were sick, I went to his house and took his temperature. And if he'd got no temperature, then he was kicked out on the spot!' Then he's back to his social partnership manner. 'Once we've got a bit more used to one another, then we'll know what we think of each other, and if we sit down together again in December – if we're still together then – for a little Christmas party, then we can perhaps sign permanent contracts. That's how we have to do it. Everything's clear now! You're a team now and I don't want to hear any more complaints about money. And you can do overtime tomorrow and Saturday, you'll have all the hours you want!'

'So, that's it,' he dismisses his men. 'Tomorrow morning, be on time. Have a good wash, clean face, and nice and fresh round the bottom too, ha ha . . .' And he shouts after Mustafa, 'Has Mustafa paid for his own beer? I don't want to end up paying for an evening's drinking.'

'So, that's it all wrapped up,' he says to Wormland, his future brother-in-law, deputy and confidant. He tells me to put his briefcase in the car, and explains to Wormland, 'Ali is my bodyguard now. Just let the boys know that. He's a karate expert and has a gun.' (I had only shown him a flick-knife.) 'Ali sat behind me the whole time and kept an eye on me. Two of them came and wanted money right away. For a moment, I really thought I was going to be for it.' Wormland answers, somewhat amused, 'I've heard you want to register them all now?' Adler winks and says, 'Well, we don't have to take everything too literally. The main thing is that there'll be peace and quiet for a while.' Suddenly, Adler shrinks back into the corner at the end of the bar as a young couple comes into the pub. The man looks angrily at Adler; the blonde, pretty woman firmly looks the other way. 'Watch out, you might have to defend me now,' Adler says to Ali, and boasts to Wormland, 'You know, I'm well known as a big stud round here.' However, his fears are unfounded, there is no argument.

Later, he tells a business friend in the pub about his 'works meeting'. 'I really beat them down on the hourly rates, so now they're really hot for overtime and double shifts. I sent them all home after that, so that they don't get talking to each other too much. You've really got to keep your eye on them all the time.'

Walter, a new German worker, has positioned himself at the other end of the bar. He's drinking one beer after another and is obviously trying to attract Adler's attention by raising his glass to him from time to time. Adler however seems to find this an annoyance and quite deliberately ignores him. After Walter, in his mid-20's, very pale and thin, has tanked himself up with ten beers, he approaches Adler, and literally pleads with him in an insistent and much too loud voice. 'Mr Adler, give me a chance, please, give me a chance. I started my apprenticeship with a company as a fitter, then I fell ill, and just before the exam I chucked it in, I admit that. I wasn't married yet then, now I've got two children who have to be fed. In my second job, I had to keep running after my money.' And imitating his former boss, he shouts, ' "You can't do your work," he shouted at me, "you're only after my money." And my next job was at a shipbuilding company, it went bust after my initial training. I've always bucked out but I've got plenty of skills. I've got all my welder's certificates, I can even do dry galvanizing, I can work accurately from drawings. Please give me a chance, and give me some other work, some skilled work. I can't feed my family on 6 or 7 marks an hour and pay the rent.'

Adler quite obviously finds it tiresome to be talked at in his free time, and after Walter has had 15 beers. He fobs him off, 'Just turn up on time tomorrow,' and, accusingly, 'Why weren't you at work today?'

Walter (upset, stuttering): 'But I told you earlier, my wife was taken to hospital, she had an operation.'

Adler (waving him away): 'First of all turn up on time every day, then we can talk about it again.'

Walter: 'Yes you can rely on me, I get up every morning at three o'clock, I come by bike, nothing can happen to me, I'll always turn up, I ride 30, 40 kilometres every day. I won't let you down.' And again and again, like a record on which the needle has stuck, 'Please, give me a chance!'

Adler, for whom Walter is becoming more and more of an annoyance, turns his back, with the words, 'If someone's always on time and does his work, he'll get his money, there's no way round that.' He turns to Wormland.

Later, Walter speaks to me in the toilet. 'You know, your boss won't let me down, he isn't really as bad as you told me on the first day.' I leave him his illusions and say nothing. Then he adds, 'Did you see how surprised he was when he saw that I'm wearing the same suit as he is!' Again, I don't have the heart to tell him the truth. Both, it is true, are wearing blue pin-striped suits. But Adler's is an extremely expensive, tailor-made one, while Walter's is a cheap off-the-peg imitation. After the eighteenth beer, Walter, who has specially put on a white shirt and a tie to grab his last chance, as if it's a job interview, realizes that Adler doesn't want to talk to him. He leaves the pub and shakily cycles the 15 kilometres home.

Adler, meanwhile, has reached beer number 20 and got into a serious argument with Wormland. Before his twentieth beer he could still produce pithy and coherent sentences and lay down business strategies like, 'We must get on the right track now,' and 'I treat my managers like precious stones,' and 'Make a plan to see how we can minimize costs.' Now Adler attacks Wormland more and more violently because he has dared to contradict him. Wormland: 'You can't treat people like that. If H.' (he mentions the name of a former German worker) 'takes you to court, he's right. I would have done the same long ago, if I wasn't related to you.' Adler, excited, replies, 'You're a traitor. You're siding with these labourers, these idlers, these robbers. You're siding with that rabble. You should stay with them!' Wormland is completely calm. I never particularly liked him when I was on the job myself, but here he suddenly shows something approaching character. At any rate, he lets Adler feel his contempt and doesn't back down. He cold-shoulders Adler, becomes more formal while he's speaking, in order to keep his distance, and replies, 'I'm not on their side, but if someone is demanding what's due to them . . .'

Adler can't bear being contradicted. 'You're dead, you're sacked. You can report in Hanover tomorrow for repair work.' Wormland says, 'I'm not doing that. I'll stay at Thyssen. You can't do without me. You can't get rid of me.' He's probably hinting that he knows a bit about Adler's workings and dirty tricks. Adler, who's red with anger, announces Wormland's dismissal or punishment transfer to the Ruhr Coal plant in Hanover several times, but Wormland remains quite cool. He is not about to lose his work at Thyssen.

At beer number 25, Adler reaches his sentimental phase, and stares at Ali with glassy eyes: 'Ali, he'll stand by me. He would lay down his life for me.' And with grandiose pathos he adds, 'I'm going to take him out of his misery. Out of his dirty hole in Diesel Street. I'll give him new clothes, so that he really goes with my Mercedes.' He is himself moved by such a demons-tration of generosity, and ponders further. 'If I only knew how to judge Ali intellectually.' He throws me an encouraging glance. I pretend I don't know what he's talking about. 'Do you know what I mean? Do you know what 'intellectual' means?'

'Yes,' I say, 'when understand everything and follow things.'

'Yeah, at what level you are. You know what I mean by level?'

'Yes,' I reply, '. . . depends where job. Most can do much more than allowed to do.'

Wormland then gets a word in to Adler: 'You can tell he doesn't get it, he expresses himself badly and speaks so slowly.'

Adler tries to play us off against one another. 'But those are the after-effects of the drugs they tried out on him. He's not so stupid at all, and understands much more than you think.'

'I not always say what think,' I support Adler, 'but often understand more than say.'

For a moment, Adler looks at me with watery eyes, scrutinizing me as if he's searching for some deeper meaning. But he seems to be satisfied when I continue, 'I not know if always understand everything right, cannot know everything, but ask maybe and see!'

Adler thinks for a minute, in order to make up his own IQ test for Ali. 'Who is the Colossus of Rhodes?' is his first question. I deliberately give him a wrong answer, so that I'm testing him, and pretend to mix up one of the seven wonders of the world with Atlas, the bearer of the heavens. 'He must carry whole world on shoulder,' I answer, 'is very heavy, is bent down and can hardly manage.'

'Good. Right. Excellent,' Adler praises me, and doesn't seem to know himself. His second question, 'What is the name of the West German Chancellor?' is answered correctly by Ali, as is, 'What was the previous one called?' And Ali also knows the name of the Soviet Communist Party Secretary. Even the name of the French President, to Adler's astonishment, comes out like a shot. 'You know quite a lot,' Adler confirms admiringly. He sees his slave workers as semi-savages, ape men and subhuman, and feels himself to be intellectually and culturally worlds above them. A few places along the bar, a 50-year-old tax officer is getting worked up about Adler's interrogation. 'What's the point of these childish questions!' Adler responds with considerable annoyance. 'I'm having a business conversation here. I won't put up with these comments.' And the examination goes on: 'Who is the Prime Minister of North Rhine Westphalia?' I tell him. 'Right! And the Minister of the Environment?' With that, he puts me in a corner. I know Klaus Matthiessen from some joint meetings in Schleswig-Holstein, and value him as one of the more progressive SPD politicians. Perhaps it's a trick question and he'll become suspicious if I know the name of a convinced left-winger. I take the precaution of saying, 'Here, not know,' and Adler dismisses it, saying, 'You don't need to know him either, you can forget him, he's one of these do-gooders, who only cause us problems. His predecessor, Bäumer, he's been a good friend of mine for years. He's got his feet on the ground and knows what's good for business. He came to my party on my last birthday. You can rely on him!' (It's useful to know who Adler's political 'godfathers' are. As the long-serving party chairman in the lower Rhine district, Bäumer was

well-known for plotting against progressive elected officials in
his own party.)

Adler is by no means a particularly colourful or unusual
bloom in our social landscape. He is respectable and recognized.
People who know him closely, know very well how he earns his
money. The more 'unpleasant' aspects of it are generously
overlooked. In such circles, once you've reached a certain size,
'one doesn't talk about money any more, one just has it'. I'm
sure Mr Bäumer has never sat down and discussed with Adler
where his money comes from, or at whose expense, and
involving what kind of crimes. You know it, keep it to yourself,
and together cultivate the pleasanter sides of life, in clubs or on
yachts. Or sometimes on holidays together, in Hawaii perhaps,
one of Adler's favourite holiday haunts. In the Ruhr, an SPD
membership is good for business and a career. I am certain that
if he lived in Bavaria, Adler would be a CSU supporter.

On another occasion, Adler boasted of having spent 200,000
marks on bribes in the last five years to get particular contracts.
But normally such direct slush-money is hardly necessary.
Often enough, all that's needed for the jobs and contracts to be
passed from one to another is the old boys' network. That's one
reason why Adler is also a member of the exclusive Düsseldorf
Golf Club where he was sponsored by a high-ranking civil
servant.

'If you give a good account of yourself,' says Adler to Ali, 'I'll
promote you.' When Ali looks at him, uncomprehending, he
makes himself clear, 'You must do everything and carry out
what I tell you, and a little bit more as well.' Ali still doesn't
understand. 'You must get a grip of your Turkish mates. You get
on well with them. You have to keep tabs on them, and tell me if
someone's talking behind my back and stirring things up. Then
he'll be kicked out before he knows what's happening. Before
one rotten apple can spoil all the others. By themselves, the boys
are more or less good-natured, but you just can't let them out of

your sight. If I only knew whether you're up to the job.'

I feel quite weak. Under no circumstances do I want to take the deception that far. It'll soon be time for me to find a way out of the situation. I'm now in a very difficult position with my colleagues and friends. And winking won't help me any more either. An informant, almost a spy: that's the part Adler has in mind for me. At the same time, I'm to remain his tame gorilla, his bodyguard. 'If it's necessary, you've got to crack down hard sometimes, so keep up your karate training.' He tries to tempt me further. 'If it works out, I'll give you a small flat quite close to me, and later you'll get a car as well. All you've got to do is stay near me and be on call any time. Diesel Street isn't a place for you. You'll go to the dogs there.' He senses my reluctance, and adds, 'You won't be let loose on your countrymen right away. At the moment I've got less bother with them than I have with some Germans who are fucking things up. There are a couple who have actually dared to take me to court to get at my money. I'll send you there, and you'll *deal* with them. Do you get me? These fucking pigs dare to tell lies about me in front of a court. You'll go there and *deal* with them, until they withdraw the case.'

He gives me the names and addresses of the two German workers, who haven't been with him for some time. I try to explain to him that in the karate club we have to sign a declaration saying that we will only make use of our training in emergencies. 'That's right, it's an emergency, I have to defend myself. They're threatening me, and you have to protect me.'

When I still look sceptical, he gives way a little. 'Just leave it for the moment. There are laws in this country after all. I've got very good lawyers, so we'll let the courts have their say first. But if I don't get my rights, then I have no choice. Then you'll have to go and sort them out. The law's completely on my side.'

Jürgen K., 26, is one of the pair who are to be *dealt* with if Adler doesn't get what he calls 'his rights'. I (as Ali) get in touch with him a little later to warn him, and learn that things have been hardly better for him as a German than for my immigrant workmates. Jürgen was unemployed for over a year, had lost his previous job because of slipped discs, and had applied in vain for work at all the big companies in the neighbourhood, including Thyssen. In response to an advert, he contacted Adler.

'At the very beginning, he didn't really make a bad impression, didn't ask any more questions, and made lots of promises. All he asked me was, "Trade union member? No? Good. Then there's no problem." He then said, "Let's see how the work comes along," or 'We'll manage to agree about that, anyway. There's no messing about, if you work well, you've got to be paid well."

'What kind of wages did I have in mind? I thought about 13 marks 50, gross. Then he said to me, that was too much, that was a wage for a skilled worker! And since I was coming from another trade, he couldn't pay me that. "Would you be willing to agree to 9 marks, net?" he asked me. I thought for a moment: 9 marks, net, is almost 13 marks 50, gross. So I said OK. "Then you can start for me on 24 January!" I was determined to be on the cards, because of pension, insurance and everything. He insisted however, "It's not worth registering you just for that short time until 1 February." So I had to work seven days in January off the books.'

Jürgen learned a month later that he'd still not been registered when he asked for a treatment certificate for his sick daughter at the local health insurance office. Adler couldn't get round that and registered him with the insurance office the same day, 25 February. Because of a clause that allows companies to register employees retrospectively up to one month after they've started work, vultures like Adler can afford to wait till something – accident or illness – happens before registering their employees. They pretend that the employee has only just started or has been employed for only a few days.

'I only slowly began to realize what a crook Adler is,' Jürgen related. 'I'm not a slacker. I really got stuck in. What do you get at the end of it? Only 5.91 marks an hour, and no overtime, no nightshift bonus, no holiday pay. It's a complete joke. And then the wage slip wasn't even right . . .

' "Yes, normally your money's there on the 15th," Adler told me. "Open a bank account, I don't pay cash." I went to the bank and opened an account. Come the day, there was no money there, on the 16th, still no money. I phoned up Adler. What's happened to the money? Yes, he says, it's already gone, it should be there by now. Today or tomorrow it would be there. I went there again, and on the next day again. By that time I didn't have any money left for petrol. My fiancée had been driving me to work. There wasn't a penny for travelling costs. Then my fiancée rang him. "Mr Adler, there's no money in the account yet!" He just laughed at her over the phone. "But nothing's going to arrive at the bank!" "What?" she says, "nothing's going to arrive at the bank?" "Yeah," he says, "one of your husband's workmates has the money!" "Why?" asks my fiancée. "I gave it to him, but you won't get him today – he's working late!"

'So right away I ran all over the steel mill, like a madman, looking for Walter who had the wages packet. It was Adler's future brother-in-law who was running around with my money. I found him as he was leaving – it wasn't even true that he was working late, he was finished at 2 pm on the dot. I said, "Walter, have you got my wage packet?" "Yes," he said, and gave me a slip, "Sign it!" "No," I said, "first of all, I've got to check it." There were 610 marks in it for February. He had paid for 79 hours, but at only 9 marks, gross, an hour! And I had worked for 126 hours! More than forty hours were missing! So I lost my temper and said, "I won't take that!" "Next month, you'll get the rest," he promised me, "and more pay."

'And the next month it was the same story again.

'They can do what they like with us. I was blackmailed: either you do a double shift or you don't need to bother coming back tomorrow. Or, I would arrive at the steel mill and the chargehand would say, "Did the boss not phone you? We don't need you today." So I had to go home again. Or the other way round: I come home at 11 o'clock at night from a double shift at Thyssen, and there's a train ticket from Adler waiting for me. I got to go up to Hamburg immediately, the train's leaving at 12.30 at night. Arrive in Hamburg at seven o'clock – no reclining seats, and I couldn't sleep in the train, it was too crowded – worked eight hours without a break at BAT, a cigarette factory, and got sent back to Duisburg. So I'd been on my feet for 26 hours, without an hour's sleep.'

Jürgen showed me all his time slips, signed by the various chargehands or foremen. During March, he constantly worked shifts of 16 hours, $17\frac{1}{2}$ hours, 14 hours and $20\frac{1}{2}$ hours, 'all without a break'.

Sometimes he was generously allowed to sleep for a couple of hours. For example, on 12 March he worked from 6 am to 10 am (16 hours), went home and slept $1\frac{1}{2}$ hours. At 12.30 am a new shift began; he worked till 9 pm the next day ($20\frac{1}{2}$ hours). Two days later, another double shift from 4 pm through to 2 pm (22 hours). On 18 March, a shift from 6 am to 2 pm (normal eight hours), home by 3.30. He slept till 8 pm ($4\frac{1}{2}$ hours). Quickly ate something. New shift began at 9.30 pm through till 7 am ($9\frac{1}{2}$ hours); slept from 8.30 am to 2 pm ($5\frac{1}{2}$ hours), and worked again from 4 pm till 2 pm (22 hours).

'We clenched our fists in our pockets,' said Jürgen. 'But I did have work, I thought. It would be even worse to have no work. If the foreman needed someone and asked, "Listen, can you work longer?" I always said straight away, "Yes if you've got something for Saturday and Sunday. I'm earning so little, I've got to do the shifts, otherwise I won't have enough money." Most of the others, the Turks – Adler had almost only Turks – were even worse off than I was. They were simply told, you work longer! If you don't want to do it, don't bother coming back tomorrow.

Tomorrow? You can go right now!'

Only very occasionally did Jürgen get to see his boss. 'He makes himself scarce and stays out of the way, basically because he's cheating everybody. I say him once when I was hired, once on a building site, and once when he appeared in court. He only calls when he wants something from you, when he wants to give you your sentence. "You've got to work tonight. Special shift again." He never says "can you", it's always "you have to". If you say "no", then you know what that means – out you go. It wasn't a job, it was like punishment for child-murderers,' is what Jürgen feels.

'We were working in the heat exchanger. The coils had to be cleaned out. Incredibly hot and dusty. Poisonous alkali dusts. Three of us were at it all day. The Thyssen workers asked us, "What's going on? Is nobody ever going to relieve you?" It was about 30° to 40°C. And if you were close to the coils, it was even hotter than that. We cleaned out the coils by hand, you've got to beat the stuff out with iron bars. Slag remnants which normally go out through the chimney had liquefied and then stuck there.

'The stuff was sticking hard. And it was right under the ingot heating furnace. If you spent 16 hours working in that heat, you really felt it! On one shift there were three of us. The other two were at the first aid station twice and I was there once; our eyes were so inflamed with all the dust in there. No masks, only face masks, not proper ones. On top of that, there's no proper ventilation, the air and all the dirt stay put, and you can't be running outside every two minutes. And above all, the job has to be finished by two o'clock, then the thing gets filled with gas. We worked there like animals. Once it was 36 hours' work over two days, on different jobs all the time. One day in the heat under the furnaces, then the next day out in the open in the middle of winter when it was minus 20°C. We had to snap off the icicles. The constant changes in temperature played hell with my discs. Some days I was on my knees because of the pains in my back, but I needed the money. Then, another time in winter, we were on a kind of platform, it was full of coal sludge, and we had to clean the belts which carry the coke. I could hardly move any more. A Turkish colleague slipped and broke his arm. After six weeks they had him working flat out again. Nobody took his injury into account.

'My biggest mistake was to leave mining. I used to work down a coal mine. And earned my money more quickly and more easily. The mine's a gift by comparison! Working underground is a holiday job compared to that! Now and then you have to put your back to it, if there's a difficult patch – but at Thyssen it was one never-ending difficult patch. Everything is done by hand. For example, we had to move the heaviest iron ingots, because we were cheaper than the cranes.'

With all of Adler's constant excuses, Jürgen was paid 861 marks for nine weeks' hard labour. He couldn't feed his family (two young children) any more. His mother went cleaning for him, 'otherwise we would really have had to starve. I got into debt. Debts here, debts there, I've still got debts.'

Jürgen was forced to go to the local welfare office. 'At first I got 500 marks a month, but I'm supposed to pay that back again. They say I've been working. Tell me, how am I supposed to pay it back?'

As early as February, Jürgen saw through the humiliating game. He told Adler that he intended to give in his notice. Adler, however, made new promises. 'I tell him, if things go on like this, then I'm throwing in the sponge. So he says "Come on, you know what, I'll give you 12 marks, net." I said, "That's just words, let's go and collect it next Monday." He said, "Sure, you'll get it in your hand. And the rest will be paid to you as well." I never saw the money.'

By 20 March, Jürgen had had enough.

'I gave my notice by phone, and the next day in writing, adding that if my wages didn't come I would take the case to the labour court. No response. I tried to phone him again, got the answering machine, gave my message, no response. A couple of days later, I phoned him again; he only asked, "Who's there?" I said, "Jürgen K . . ." He said "Talk to my lawyer". So I went to court. Labour court. The first hearing – that was terrible. First of all, it was beneath Adler himself to turn up at all. And then I ended up feeling as if I was being accused. The hearing lasted two and a half minutes. And then I was outside again. All they said was: you've named the wrong company! I asked why. Adler-Heisterkamp Ltd doesn't exist, there's only an Adler Ltd in Oberhausen. "Wait a minute," I say, "I have a wage slip here from Adler-Heisterkamp Ltd." But what was I supposed to do? If you're not familiar with the law, and haven't got a lawyer, you're lost. A guy like that only needs a bankruptcy and he's solved his problems again for a while. So I got a lawyer, but that costs money too. I probably won't even get legal costs because I was working. It will cost at least 1,000 marks. After that's paid, there'll probably only be a few hundred marks left over from the compromise agreed. An unscrupulous business-man like Adler always cuts a better figure, even in court.

'At the final hearing, he actually arrived in person and wanted to finish me off. He claimed I was a liar, a cheat, and that the time slips were forged. All my time slips were signed by the foreman, and in duplicate, one copy for Remmert and one for me. That's where it got out, that during March – in February I hadn't cottoned on yet – I had worked 129 hours, and that was only up to 20 March, which included a stretch when I was on my feet for 36 hours non-stop. But on my tax card, which he had to produce in court, only 434 marks, gross, were recorded. And no company stamp. He had embezzled the rest. In court he behaved as if he was the chief judge. He got a warning, and then he let loose a stream of abuse about lay judges. An employer was guilty from the start, one accepts one's guilt, because you don't get any justice anyway. Or, as he said to me, "Swindler! Forger!"

'My lawyer advised a compromise because the case would have gone on for months, perhaps years. And I needed the money. Instead of the outstanding 2,735 marks, calculated on the basis of an hourly rate of 9.50 marks – because everything else had only been promised by him verbally, not in writing – I accepted back pay of 1,750 marks.

'Then after the hearing, I had to send the tax card to him again. It's not back yet, almost a month later. And not a penny of the settlement either. Now he's got to make up the insurance and pension contributions, and he's taking his time about it. The labour court treats him like an honest man who's a little muddled. And people like us are the losers!

'The employers can do what they like nowadays. And especially these subcontractors. There are too many unemployed. And too few people who open their mouths against this kind of thing!'

Jürgen couldn't start a new job, because Adler, true to form, didn't give him back his tax card.

'I was without a tax card and without an insurance card for the whole of April and for half of May as well. I spoke to the Remmert company about being taken on. They said, good, you can start with us, but you must bring along your cards, then everything's OK. Yeah, well, I didn't have the cards, because Adler had them. Then I went and got a temporary tax card, and brought the temporary card to Remmert. He says, "No, we can't accept that, you worked for us, so you must have the original tax card." I'm sure it's just an excuse, they're hand in glove with Adler.

'In my opinion Mr Adler got off far too lightly. He's already pulling in the next lot, there it is in the paper again: "Adler Industrial Repairs is looking for . . ." I just don't know how he does it, how he keeps people working for him – I don't understand it! At the labour court he admitted quite candidly, "I have never employed anyone for more than 9 marks, gross." '

There's one small comfort for Jürgen. 'There are foreigners who are even worse off. He had Pakistanis working for him for 6 marks, gross. They didn't have residence permits.'

Adler's practices and the serious risks of the work are also demonstrated by the following statements from Turkish workers:

Hüseyin Atsis, aged 56, who had already done the worst kinds of dirty work in Turkey has the feeling that 'Siberia must be better than this job'. He had 'never seen such dangerous workplaces' before. 'In the newly constructed furnace at Hamborn, we had to drag these pipes down from the seventh floor. There were two of us to each pipe. We had to be careful doing it, because we knew we were risking our lives. On another job, we had to climb 70 metres up a crane and sweep up dust and then get the 50 kilogram sacks down to the ground. It was very dangerous and very dirty. I asked the foreman why I always had to do this kind of work. He said, "At least you're insured, you've got your cards. If something happens, then something can still be done for you." He told me that Adler has very few workers who are legally employed, only a couple who are properly insured.'

Hüseyin Atsis had to run after his money, too. When eventually, after constantly asking, he received a series of long drawn-out partial payments, the total was far below what he could have expected on the basis of the agreed hourly rate and the regular overtime. Instead of the 10 marks an hour that had been agreed, only 9 marks had been allowed for, and also, there were unexplained deductions. For 184 working hours, Hüseyin received only 724 marks, 28 pfennigs. 'When I got the money, I said to myself, you can't get into a fight with these people. And then perhaps they'll really do you harm and get you expelled. So I said, It's best if I just try to get my cards from them and forget the money. But he said to me, "I'm not giving you your cards. First of all you have to sign that you've received everything that's due to you. Only if you do that will I hand over your papers." '

Sait Tümen, aged 25, and Osman Tokar, aged 22, had similar experiences. Sait Tümen told me: 'I had already been working for Adler for three months, and during that whole time he never gave me a proper pay packet, sometimes only 100 marks or 200 marks. But I worked almost every day. I was always borrowing money from friends in order to live and saying, "You'll get it back right away, as soon as I get my money from Adler." He had said I was quite certain to get it in a few days. When I couldn't pay back my debts to my friends they thought I was cheating them, and didn't talk to me any more. So I lost my friends. I then tried to find work elsewhere. But they wanted my cards, otherwise there was no work. So I went to Adler and told him I'd got new work, but only if I got my papers, and that I wanted the rest of my money. But Adler said, "You only get your cards if you sign that you don't want any more money from me." I thought about it. If I didn't hand in the cards in the next few days, there'd be no new job. What could I do? My new boss was a good friend of Adler's! So I signed for Adler that I was to get no more money. The slip was already typed out. He had lots of them. It said: Acknowledgement. I hereby acknowledge that I have no further claims arising from my limited contract with Adler Industrial Repairs Ltd.'

Osman Tokar told me: '*Adler always deducted a couple of hours every week, and we went to see him about it. He said we'd get the remainder with the next payment, but it wasn't there. So we went to him again, he always said next time, next time, he always chases us away with that. When I went to see him again, he said to me: "If you don't want to work at 9 marks with 40 per cent deductions, then I will put an advert in the WAZ,* and there'll be a thousand people at the door the very next day. You're foreigners," he said, "be satisfied that you've got work at all."* '

Osman also reported working conditions which were hazardous to health. '*We had to work in a plant where you could hardly see because of all the dust, and we couldn't breathe properly anymore. After a few days, I had terrible pains, a stabbing pain in my heart and in my lungs. A worker from Thyssen came and told me that the iron dust was very dangerous, even deadly, and that I should get a dust mask from the boss. So I went to the Thyssen foreman, but he didn't give me a mask. He said it wasn't so bad at all, I shouldn't make such a fuss, but should finish the job off quickly. He*

---

* WAZ, *Westdeutsche Allgemeine Zeitung*, a local Ruhr daily. (Trans.)

really put pressure on us; if we weren't finished within 20 hours, we'd just have to stay there and keep going. We wouldn't be allowed to leave.

After work, I immediately went to the doctor. I had a terrible cough. The doctor examined me and right away asked where I was working. I said at Thyssen, for a contractor, and then he asked me where my workplace was, if there was gas or iron dust or something else that was bad for the lungs. So I told him that there was iron dust there. Then he said I wasn't the only one from Thyssen coming to him with these problems. If I really wanted to be healthy, I should find another job. He prescribed me some drugs.

13. RADIATION

I'm now lined up for a spell of work in Würgassen nuclear power station. It's the oldest nuclear power station in West Germany, having been operational since 1971, and requires a lot of repair work. Reliable workers are needed for the annual maintenance. Immigrants, especially Turks, are preferred. I assume it's because they're so 'mobile'.

In West Germany there is no precise information on the consequences of limited doses of radiation. Most foreign workers who are sent into the intensively radioactive areas of nuclear power stations in repair or cleaning gangs, don't appear in the statistics years or decades later if they have developed cancers of the testicles, the prostate or the thyroid. By that time, they are living in other cities, or have returned to their faraway homes, and nobody is interested in the work they once did in a German nuclear power station. It's for this reason that the managements of the nuclear power stations try to make do with a small, permanent, full-time staff, and for the relatively dangerous jobs, they often hire temporary workers from subcontractors. Often, these temporary workers receive the maximum 'allowable' annual radiation dose of 5,000 milliremes in a few hours or days, or sometimes even within a few seconds. I talked to German and Turkish workers who did this work for 10 marks an hour!*

---

* The comments by those affected and by informants have been made in the form of sworn statements.

A former worker reports: 'When there are breakdowns, then usually the Turks are sent in. They are sent into the contaminated, hot area to stop the gap, and have to stay there until they've been exposed to doses of 5,000 milliremes. That may take hours, but in some cases it's only minutes or even seconds. The workers call it 'burning up'.* Normally, those affected are then 'banned' for the rest of the year.'

'But there are ways,' one worker explains to me, 'of working somewhere else,' (i.e. in another power station). He won't say how. In order to experience these possibly lethal working conditions myself, and to be able to prove convincingly that they do exist, I have made a job application to Würgassen. The problem is that they carry out a security check first. I have given the name and address of my double, together with all his places of residence during the last ten years, so that the Office for the Defence of the Constitution** can get to work. The computers bring their elephantine memories into operation: Participation in demonstrations? Other activities? The Federal Criminal Office is also brought in. Normally such a check takes six weeks, in exceptional cases, it's up to three months. In my case – that is to say, in the case of my double – more detailed research seems to be necessary, since after two months there is neither a positive nor a negative response. Perhaps because it's holiday time. In any case, I take the opportunity to approach the problem differently than originally planned. (A doctor friend, a radiographer and radiation expert, whom I had told about my plan to do 'Turk's work' in the nuclear power station, emphatically warned me against it. My state of health – chronic bronchitis

---

* Scientists independent of the nuclear power industry fear that maximum doses received in such a short time can produce radiation cancer as a long-term effect. (When X-ray technology began, the supposedly tolerable maximum levels were also set far too high).

** The name of the internal security force in West Germany. (Trans.)

resulting from the Thyssen dust and also a general debility as a result of the drug experiment – was already quite poor.)

I'm not exactly full of the joys of life. On the contrary, I feel pretty washed out. I identify with my role, and the almost hopeless situation of my workmates and friends depresses me more and more. However, I'm frightened by the thought of slowly wasting away, eaten up by radiation cancer in a struggle with death lasting perhaps years. So I admit that I'm a coward and that I'm in a privileged position. Hundreds and thousands of immigrant workers who get the chance are forced to put their health, perhaps even their lives, at risk, even if, physically, they're in a much worse condition than me. The attractive part of the work is that it doesn't usually involve physical exertion, so older workers, the ill and the worn out, can cope with it.

In addition, most immigrants aren't even informed about the special dangers involved in this kind of work. When I applied to Würgassen, I made a point of asking, 'Is work not dangerous?' The personnel manager assured me, 'It's no different from anywhere else in industry!'

What the work in Würgassen is really like is documented by a number of witnesses. Frank M. is a chargehand in Würgassen:

'On the one hand, it's a job where you can quickly and easily earn money. As a chargehand I had 2,500 marks net on my last pay slip. On the other hand, I would not work more than five years there. Even if I was to lose my job. After five years, I'd rather sign on as unemployed. The radiation level is far too high, the plant is far too old. It's a boiling water reactor, and they have even higher radiation than the pressurized water reactors. In my opinion, every cup of coffee you drink there is contaminated. Just going in, you've already got 10 milliremes on the dosimeter, even before you've begun to work.'

The dosimeter is a measuring instrument which everyone in the 'hot area' has to wear. It shows the radiation which has built up at the workplace in the course of a day. However, fear of not being able to clock up enough hours often leads to the instrument being doctored. A former Würgassen worker explains:

'You're in charge of it yourself. You put the dosimeter down somewhere, in your locker, for instance, and nobody notices. Nobody bothers about it. During the whole time that I worked here in Würgassen, nobody asked me for it. It can't register what's not there . . . I know about a case involving the subcontractors, Reinhold and Mahler. They had a whole gang of Yugoslavs working, about 16 men. They were all there illegally, without cards. They often don't take the security regulations seriously. When that was found out, they had to go. They were got rid off very discreetly. In Grohnde, for example, no more than 20 per cent of the welders are Germans. The rest are all foreigners.'

Frank M. continues: 'Our sub-company has about 2,500 people. At least 1,500 of them are foreigners. They simply do their job, and when the maintenance is over, they're dismissed. Most of them are only there for a couple of weeks. These are the people who are put most at risk. They come in and get a certain amount of radiation. In the company I work for, there are site foremen and chargehands who are normally there for longer. All the rest are there for only a short time. If they've got a limited contract, for example, for a maintenance job, and they've received their allowed three month dose within two weeks, then the radiation safety in the plant says they're not allowed in any more and they're dismissed. We also have a lot of Turks, who are flown here specially from Turkey on short contracts, and they do welding till they've reached the limit of their dose. If welders are required and they have to work in a high radiation area, where, let's say, there's an hourly dose of 1,000 milliremes, then they work for two hours before being replaced and sent home. Then the next lot come in, they work for another two hours till they've got 2,000, and then they've got to go home too. There is constant turnover till the job's done.

'When the foreign workers come they don't even know why they have to stop after two days or after two hours. They're only told they're prohibited, and that they've got to leave and go home.'

Frank M. has this to say about the work of cleaners on the reactor basin: 'When the plant is shut down, about 30 per cent of the fuel rods, on average, are replaced. They get put in the basin. They stay there for one year till the radiation level goes down. When the rods are replaced, the water leaks and there are always some of our people there who have to keep the floor around the basin clean, so that contamination doesn't spread to the rest of the plant. While one person works in the basin, another one holds him, secured by a cable. If someone falls into the water, he has to be pulled out again within ten seconds, because you can't swim in that water.'

The Yugoslav worker, Dragan V.: 'When I was hired, they didn't say anything to me about the danger from radiation. All they said to me was, your quarterly permissible dose is 2,500 millirems, annual 5,000. That's all they said. How dangerous it is, nobody said anything about that.'

On 20 August 1982, 14 workers from outside companies were so seriously contaminated while replacing a 'sand filter' in the off-gas system that they had to be taken to the radiation clinic in Düsseldorf. The plant management ordered strict silence on the case. Here is the report of a worker who was present in Würgassen when the accident took place:

'I'm always frightened when I'm working in there. Especially since the accident. On that occasion, first of all, they decided to set a time limit. So the people had to keep working inside for another half hour. Then all of a sudden the area was completely closed. The polishers were more than 20 feet down. The others had all been sitting in the stairwell. There was a room leading off that – that's where all the stuff came down. They had their toolboxes in the room, and there were cables running out of it, so of course, the door was open. They didn't even notice anything until the complete closure was ordered. They wanted to go through the automatic checks, through the monitors that measure the radiation levels at the exit. That's when they found out that they were completely contaminated.

'Then everything started. They had to shower again and again, but it didn't make any difference. The rest of us were already outside, and they were still in the showers. They showered until three in the afternoon, and almost scrubbed their skins off. From half-past eleven. And they came out at three again. Only the machine house and the railtrack entrance were still closed. On the next day, Saturday, we were working again, we wanted to make up the hours. All the men who had been contaminated arrived and showered again till midday. From seven in the morning until twelve. But their levels did not go down. Then on Monday they were sent off to Düsseldorf radiation clinic. But they only carried out measurements there, no treatment. Nearly all of the contaminated workers were barred for the rest of the year.'

A German worker, Horst T., also had an accident: 'One day, when I was in the condensation chamber, I tore my protective suit. When, on my way out, I passed the monitors the whole box lit up from top of bottom. I thought, that's impossible! So I showered for almost two hours. Again and again: shower, monitor, shower, monitor. I didn't even bother drying my hair. It gets into the pores, and you can scrub at it for hours. They told me I had received about 2,800 milliremes in total. But how do I know it wasn't many times that amount? Then they sacked me. Lack of work, apparently. They said I wasn't suitable for this kind of job. I wanted to have my radiation pass which lists the doses you have recieved. I eventually got it after a lot of effort, but there was nothing on it. I was told I should send it to Kassel, to the subcontractor. So I did that. And after a fortnight they rang me up, to see if I wanted to start again. Now I've got a new radiation pass. I had to sign for it, and nothing had been entered, absolutely nothing. As if I had never worked there before . . .'

Very few employees ever see the radiation passes, which are required by law, and serve as evidence of contamination. The passes stay in the offices of the various subcontractors, and sometimes they disappear or are doctored before the authorities carry out inspections. In this way, the subcontractors demonstrate their own kind of responsibility for their men.

Whenever it has the opportunity, the nuclear industry minimizes the dangerous consequences of constant contact with radioactivity. For example, anyone entering the Würgassen atomic power station to work in the 'hot area' is entertained with a colour video. 'Radiation is comparable to sunlight,' announces a cheerful voice-over, and a bronzed girl lying under an open sunshade on some southern beach appears on the screen. Workers report how foremen try to dispel their fears: 'It's the same amount of radiation as you get on a fortnight's holiday at the seaside.' The cheerful slogan from Würgassen which is repeated in every 'information film' states: 'Avoid every unnecessary exposure to radiation and keep every *unavoidable* exposure to radiation as limited as possible.'

However, no one keeps track of what actually happens to the workers. The Bremen radiation researcher, Professor Inge Schmitz-Feuerhake: 'We know today that every dose of radiation, no matter how large or small, can cause harm, in the form of either radiation-induced cancer, or genetic damage in descendants. And the insidious thing about damage caused by radiation is that it often only appears many years, often up to 20 or 30 years, after exposure. Nuclear technology has not been in operation long enough in West Germany for its effects to be known with any certainty.'

In West Germany, the Technical Supervision Association (TÜV, Technische Überwachungsverein) is responsible for the safety of nuclear power stations. The Institute for Accident Research of the Rhineland district TÜV in Cologne passed a report, Human Factors in the Nuclear Power Station, *to the Minister of the Interior. It has never been published. In it, TÜV researchers investigate the 'problems' arising from the employment of so-called 'outside personnel' – problems for the industry, and not for the people involved: 'Problems arise, first of all, in working with untrained ancillary personnel from service companies who are employed on radiation-intensive jobs in order to conserve their permanent employees. According to the statements of management staff, these workers are often poorly motivated and reluctant to work . . .'*

No wonder! Who does enters a nuclear power station cheerfully? The report goes on: '. . . the systematic fulfilment of necessary work tasks does not permit the abandonment of outside services.' 'Personnel shortages' frequently arise 'due to dosages of radiation received and the related limited availability of the plant's permanent employees.' 'The admissible doses of radiation are often received within a very short time (a few minutes).' 'One task required of the permanent personnel is to give outside personnel appropriate instructions with speed and precision, especially on jobs exposed to radiation . . . exact instruction is often not possible or the effort is inappropriate. The employment of outside personnel is inefficient.' The TÜV report observes drily that 'the majority of outside personnel is inexperienced with regard to this risk . . . lack of knowledge of the plant and of the system is a contributing negative factor, especially since a proper supervision is not possible, given that outside personnel are being employed to conserve the plant's own personnel . . . Careless behaviour on the part of outside personnel entrusted with high radiation tasks is made more likely by a feeling of helplessness in the face of a largely unknown danger.'

Who could prove, after such a long time, that a fatal cancer was the result of such a job in the 'hot area' of a nuclear power station? The workers from subcontractors are given a medical examination before the job – but not after it. Murder by instalments? Secretly, without witnesses, without evidence, wholesale. Every year, tens of thousands of cleaners and welders work in German nuclear power stations (in Würgassen alone, up to 5,000 people were sent into the danger zone in one year). About half of them are foreign, who frequently return to their homelands before the consequences become visible or noticeable.

Only insiders and scientists are in a position to decipher reports like the one in the *Frankfurter Allgemeine* newspaper of 29 July 1982. Under the headline, A THOUSAND MEN JUST TO REPLACE THE PIPES, the paper reports on repair work in Würgassen, and mentions in the secret language of the atomic industry that 'a thousand men-rem' are to be expected during the work. 'Men-rem'? It sounds like a secret code from a spy movie, or perhaps a short-wave transmission frequency. The companies, however, know very well what it means. This mysterious unit of measurement quickly allows the professionals to calculate how many cases of cancer can be expected. The former director of radiation safety in the American atomic research centre at Oak Ridge, Carl Z. Morgan, (whom scientists call the 'father of radiation protection') says that '1,000 men-rem' means about 6 to 8 cancer deaths per thousand. Purely a matter of statistics.

14. THE CONTRACT

With adequate profit, capital is very bold. A
certain 10 per cent will ensure its employment
anywhere; 20 per cent certain will produce
eagerness; 50 per cent, positive audacity; 100
per cent will make it ready to trample on all
human laws; 300 per cent, and there is not a
crime at which it will scruple, nor a risk it will
not run, even to the chance of its owner being
hanged. If turbulence and strife will bring a
profit, it will freely encourage both. Smuggling
and the slave trade have amply proved all that
is here stated.

T.J. Dunning, 'Trades Unions and Strikes', pp. 35–6.
Quoted in Karl Marx, *Capital* Vol 1, p. 926, footnote
15 (Pelican edition 1976).

As luck would have it, Adler also has men working at Würgassen
nuclear power station. As is his usual practice, there were not
many of them. He prefers to be decentralized and inconspicuous.
Maybe 30 here, and ten there, and one over there. If things go
wrong in Hamburg, business will still keep turning over in the
Ruhr, at Thyssen, Steag, MAN and at Ruhr Coal in southern
Germany. What was his motto, again? 'Lots of chickens make
muck too'; and 'Laws are there to be got round'.

I want to try and act out just how far rapacious businessmen are prepared to go. Friends and colleagues are ready to help. The Cologne actor, Heinrich Pachl, will take the part of the nuclear power station safety officer, Schmidt, and my colleague, Uwe Herzog, that of his scientific assistant, Hansen.

The secret contract

Because of a technical failure, the Würgassen nuclear power station can't supply the national grid with electricity, which means a loss of millions. Turkish workers are required, who will climb into the contaminated zone to repair the damage. It is probable that they will receive large and concentrated doses of radiation that will cause the most serious damage to health and eventually produce cancer. The condition is that the Turks must not know anything of the risks involved, and after completion of the job must be sent back to their own country as quickly as possible. Adler, so 'Schmidt' explains, is well known in the business as an especially reliable person for this kind of job. The first contact is on the car telephone. I'm driving Adler back to Oberhausen when the call comes through.

Pachl/Schmidt: 'Yes, good afternoon. My name is Schmidt, in charge of radiation protection at Würgassen. Mr Adler, we have the following problem. I'll come straight to the point. We have an unfortunate situation there, a breakdown, which we can't deal with technologically. It occurred to me that you might be the right person to help us sort it out. We need an intensive, short–term manpower deployment. The question is this, because the matter is very urgent, whether – I'm in the neighbourhood, in the Ruhr, right now – we could meet immediately? Let's say in an hour? The motorway restaurant at Lichtendorf, between the Westhofen and Unna intersections? Let's say at half past one?'

Adler pulls the Ruhr area map out of the side pocket of the

door, and studies it thoroughly. Then he says to me, 'We must get a move on. Drive me quickly to Remmert, in Oberhausen. At half past one I have to be at the Lichtendorf motorway restaurant. A customer is waiting for me there. New job.' After Remmert, he's in a hurry. He forces me to ignore speed limits. 'Step on it, I can't afford to be late.' When, after overtaking, a woman driver doesn't pull over, Adler is beside himself with anger. 'That stupid cow, that arsehole, get right up behind her, make her move, we're going to be late.' Now, he suddenly starts talking about 'we'. We reach the restaurant five minutes late. He grabs his little case, and hurries off to the new deal, though not without first having given me a job to do. 'Take the brush and the duster out of the glove compartment and make sure everything is spotless. The ashtray as well. I don't want to see a speck of dust when I come back.' 'Of course,' I say, short and to the point. It's the answer which he, as I've found out, likes best.

It's 1.35 pm on Wednesday, 7 August, when the two power station safety officers sit down face to face with Adler for the initial conversation.

Pachl/Schmidt: 'We're under incredible pressure because we're so short of time. In fact, we have to get the whole business out of the way by Friday . . .'

Adler: 'I'm a medium-sized business. We do whatever's needed. Our customers include, for example, Ruhr Coal and Steag. We've already done a lot of work for you.'

Pachl/Schmidt: 'We've worked out two possibilities. In this case, we want eight reliable workers, who don't need to have worked in this area before . . .'

Adler: 'Fine.'

Pachl/Schmidt: 'Right, they're going to be sent in there. That's the first thing. It's possible that the problem can be cleared up very quickly, but it's also possible that it might take longer.'

After these introductory remarks, which only hint at the 'hot' contract, Adler, nevertheless, already fully grasps the situation.

He immediately emphasizes that he can 'send over eight or ten reliable people tomorrow'. Then he puts the question that shows him to be a professional in this business. 'But can we do something about the radiation passes?' Pachl/Schmidt is prepared for this and requests the first illegality. 'Without radiation passes, of course'. The breakdown must be dealt with by Friday at 1800 hours at the latest. Adler is not put out. 'Yes, without radiation passes? . . . You need eight men, tomorrow, without radiation passes. That's OK! I'm doing my job. You're doing your job. Everything top secret, etcetera, etcetera.'

Pachl/Schmidt continues with further demands. Agreement is quickly reached that only people who 'don't come from this area' should be considered, 'foreign workers' who can 'be withdrawn immediately'. And Pachl/Schmidt immediately introduces the principal reason for the quick removal of the workers. 'Of course, it's possible that something might happen . . .' At the same time he's reassuring. If something emerges, let's say, with cancer there's never just one cause . . . cancer can have a latency period of 20 years.' Adler (relieved), 'Yeah, right.' Pachl/Schmidt reasserts, 'It can never really be proved.' Then Herzog/Hansen produces drawings which can leave Adler in no doubt that he's being asked to provide a suicide squad.

Herzog/Hansen: 'Look at this. These are the pipes here. They have a diameter of 67 centimetres. The men must get in there . . .'

Adler: 'Where is . . . the reactor core . . . here?'

Herzog/Hansen: 'That's the safety pressure container. The pipes through which the radioactive steam flows onto the turbines run in between the pressure container and the machine house. And in the middle of the pipe, here, that's where our 'mouse' has got stuck.'

Adler: 'Hmm, hmm.'

Herzog/Hansen: 'Perhaps you've seen one of these 'mouse' things before; it's a small laser instrument which scans the interior of the pipe for cracks. And it is stuck here, we can't get it out, that's the problem. That's where the people would have to get to; it's not hard work, but they should be healthy.'

Adler: 'Oh they are. Yes, yes, of course.'

Herzog/Hansen: 'They have to get in there. The trouble is this: For technical reasons we can't, at the moment, say how high the radiation in that sector is. It could be damned high.'

Adler: 'Shall we provide badges or anything like that?'

Herzog/Hansen: 'We provide the dosimeters. That's not a problem. We provide protective clothing. The question is, to what extent the radiation has lodged there. We can only really assess that when they come out.'

Adler (talking like a pimp about his workers): 'Right, I've got people at Thyssen, for example, eight of them can be taken out tomorrow, I'll take the best ones. We'll be here tomorrow morning with our own transport. They are . . . foreigners. Maybe the odd German, but in the main foreigners. They'll have no idea what it's about. And after that they keep their mouths shut, and a week later they're back on board here. Is there a possibility, I mean, I'd also be interested, as a businessman, in the longer-term employment of other men. That would be really advantageous for me. Cleaning work, things like that, everything, long term . . .'

Pachl/Schmidt: 'My suggestion is this: first of all, we wrap this business up. I'm sure if it turns out to everyone's satisfaction, then we'll be happy to get in touch with you again. The other thing would be, in case, if there was, let's say, a further problem . . .'

Adler: 'Yes . . .?'

Pachl/Schmidt: 'Do you have men . . .?'

Adler: 'Of course, I've got reserves. They caan be replaced immediately.'

Pachl/Schmidt: '. . . who for one reason or another, have to go back home in the near future?'

Herzog/Hansen: 'We must be prepared for everything. The risks are large. A willingness to return to Turkey could perhaps also be made more attractive by a bonus.'

Pachl/Schmidt (who can afford to be generous with regard to the payment): 'I've still to check it out, but the total amount will be around 120,000 to 150,000 marks . . .'

Adler: 'You've explained the problems. I'm a businessman, I do whatever's required. I want to pay the rent and the men will earn their bit. Now. Who's available? Who's on the deportation list at the consulate? Who's in trouble with the aliens' department? I know all that. So, we take them. Right.'

With that, the deal is settled for Adler. He asks again for the names of the two 'safety officers': '. . . Mr Schmidt and Mr . . .?' 'Hansen,' Herzog/Hansen reminds him, and Adler believes he remembers. 'Sure, I think I've heard your name, yes, yes, from Würgassen . . .' The lucrative deal strengthens Adler's trust in them. He again assures both partners of his reliability before quickly getting back to the point once more – money.

Adler: 'I've got my men under control. When we're working for a customer, they've got to work, all right. If they hang around talking out they go. It happens elsewhere; at Thyssen, we sometimes have to do something like this. No one hears about it, not a word gets out. Right. The operation starts tomorrow, 8 August 1985. Let's just tie things up, then: how much do you want to spend?'

Pachl/Schmidt: 'Our budget is around 120 to 150,000 marks. You carry the risk for any consequences that emerge later, that's your problem. It's up to you to make sure they're far enough away.'

Adler: 'But back to another question, so that I know exactly. When they come out, they'll come out . . . injured . . . won't they?'

Pachl/Schmidt: 'I think we all know what we're doing. That's what we're paying for, after all. Normally, with this amount of contamination, we would say that it must be followed by treatment. Only in this case, that's something we can't allow, because people will start asking questions, or if someone's been here for a while he'll start talking. And we have to prevent that at all costs.'

Herzog/Hansen: 'They have to leave immediately! Immediately!'

Adler: 'That's understood ... Now, let's get this quite straight, I have the men, I get them together. Then you send them into the danger zone, right? That's no problem.'

Everything's straightforward. To send 'my men' into the 'danger zone', is 'no problem' for Adler. Only the details remain to be sorted out. Pachl/Schmidt will provide a minibus from the power station to pick up the group in Duisburg the next day. Adler explains that his regular workers at the power station are installed in the hotel Zur Kurve in Würgassen, and that he is ready to collect the money right away if possible.

They leave the restaurant together. I think I can tell from Adler's satisfied face that he has agreed to the deal. I throw open the car door for him, the way he likes me to, and without a word he pushes the button until his soft upholstered seat has been adjusted to the most comfortable and relaxed position.

'Back to Oberhausen,' is all that he says, and then he falls silent. He's thinking hard. For a little while I begin to suspect that perhaps I have done him an injustice, that he does recoil from this completely criminal job. Perhaps he's not as unscrupulous as all that. No one could be so hardboiled! He won't put any lives at risk. His workers at Thyssen are burnt out slowly and indirectly, and the concentrated heavy metal dust is like a time bomb which will eventually produce cancer in some of them. But the knowledge of that is easier to live with. Here, the situation is much more clear-cut. Workers become aware of the dust at Thyssen, even if many don't know about its effects on their health. The illness and possible death caused by radiation in the nuclear power station is not something the workers can be aware of if they're not told.

I soon learn that his thoughts are taking quite another direction. He's scribbling figures in his little notebook and seems to be calculating something. Suddenly he interrupts his silence, and says, 'Can you get hold of seven or eight of your countrymen, who want to earn a bit of money, by tomorrow morning? It'll be good work, but they must be reliable.'

I pretend to give it some thought. Adler says, 'If you can't manage it so quickly, I'll ask K. He's always got a few on hand.' K. is a Turkish worker, elevated to the role of trusty, and when Adler is at a loss as to where to get new people, K. pulls them in.

'I can,' is all I say, 'and what must people be able to do?'

'They don't need to be able to do anything special,' says Adler, 'I'm only anxious that they should be the poorest of the poor. Tell them, I was poor too, once . . .'

I look at him in astonishment. 'You were poor? When you were poor?'

'Well . . . after the war we were all poor. They can be people who are worried about being deported.' He notices my bewilderment and quickly supplies a motive. 'I want to help them because they have such a hard time here, you know. I was always socially minded. I grew up a Social Democrat.'

'What is that?' I ask.

'That's the party that's for the workers,' he informs me. 'I'm a member.'

'What is work?' I want to know. 'How much money?'

'They'll earn good money,' he says, '500 marks for two days. And the work . . . it's light cleaning work, very clean, they won't even get their hands dirty . . .'

'Where is?'

He doesn't say exactly. He even lies about that! 'It's within 60 miles.' (In fact, Würgassen is about 180 miles away.)

'It doesn't matter if some of them are without residence permits,' he continues, 'but it would be best if they go back to Turkey soon after the job is finished. If you bring me the people, you get 500 marks too.'

'Can be people from refugee hostel?'

'No, nothing to do with the authorities!' he warns me. 'You see, the money's off the books.'

'What is "off the books"?' I ask.

'Black, no taxes. I'll give it to them cash. No one needs to show cards or anything. It's all under the table, they prefer it that way. Then they've got some money for Turkey, and can do something with it. They should also take some things with them for staying the night. Underwear and so on. Everything else will be provided. Where are you going to find them?'

'I know some, they live, hide in cellar.'

'That's good,' he says, 'if they're living in a cellar, then they don't have any other contacts. How many are there, then?'

'Five, maybe . . .'

'Yeah,' he says, 'have a good look round and perhaps you can make it up to eight. Call me any time! You can reach me at the tennis club. It would be best not to bring them to my office at home, but to your flat in Diesel Street. I'll come there, and then they'll be picked up. The most important thing is that they disappear afterwards. I want to see it in writing that they will immediately leave the country. They have got to leave anyway. Isn't the police aliens' department after them?'

'Yes,' I reply, 'some for this, some for that.'

'Right, it must be clear they all have to get out! I don't want to find out that they're still around here weeks later. That's the condition for this job . . .'

I ask in more detail about the work that's to be done. But he only says, 'You won't understand it, it'll be explained to them. It's really not a problem. What's important is that these people, who have already suffered enough here, must be helped . . .'

He's talking like a clergyman, there's suddenly something unctuous in his voice. But in a second, he's his old self again. 'The main thing is, I must be able to count on you.'

'Understood,' I say.

I'm to phone him up in the evening to report the success of my mission. I reach him in the restaurant of his tennis club. He's been informed by his customer, Schmidt, that six men will be enough. (I couldn't persuade any more to participate at such short notice.)

Adler seems to have difficulty in speaking freely. In front of business friends and his employees, who know him and know what he's up to, he can hardly profess to be a benefactor of Turks, or show off his party membership, so good for business in the Ruhr, as a commitment to the 'workers' party'. It would be met by uproarious laughter.

'What shall I tell colleagues?' I cause him further embarrassment. 'I can't tell you, this minute,' he hums and haws. 'Call me at home in an hour.'

On the phone at home, his voice again takes on a pastoral note. When I insist: 'And what shall I say? Why you do this for these people?' Adler manages to heighten his charitable rhetoric. It's no longer the 'poorest of the poor', but the 'poorest of the poorest' – 'and I want to put a few pennies in their pockets'. When I interrupt and describe in detail the situation of some Turkish workers, he has difficulty concealing his indifference. It's only because he needs me to play my part in the deal, that he manages to force out, 'Well, we can talk about it,' and is even prepared, at my suggestion, to procure a work permit and flat for the 'poorest of the poorest' – knowing full well that he's promised the 'safety officer' that he'll make the foreign workers disappear when the job is done.

The next morning. 9.30 am. The power station officer, Schmidt, phones Adler to check that everything is going as planned.

Adler: 'I've got the men together, they're ready. Not tell me, fair and square, who am I dealing with? You are not Mr Schmidt from Würgassen. I already know that. Who are you? I want to know who I'm dealing with. And then we can settle the business.'

We had reckoned that Adler could enquire at Würgassen, and would then find out that the real safety officer had never left the plant. So Pachl/Schmidt had taken the precaution of explaining to Adler, 'Don't try to reach me at my office. The matter is so confidential, that I would then have to deny I knew you and would unfortunately have to tell you, "I don't know you, we've never met, and there's no such job". We are a highly sensitive security section, and the enemy's listening in everywhere, even on our own staff.' It looks as if Adler didn't find out by phoning up himself, but through a third party. But we were ready for this possibility as well.

Pachl/Schmidt: 'Now, please, set your mind at rest. The utmost discretion is called for in this case. It's too big for Schmidt to handle. The decision has been made at executive level.'

Adler: 'Right. I can understand that.'

Pachl/Schmidt: 'And discretion naturally requires a certain degree of trust . . .'

Adler: 'Right, and that's there.'

Pachl/Schmidt: 'If it's not there, I believe we should re-think everything again. We are in a situation, which for us . . .'

Adler: 'Yes . . .'

Pachl/Schmidt (raising his voice pompously): 'Precisely because we are resspsonsible for Germany's energy supply, and no other possibility whatsoever remains open to us . . .'

Adler: 'Yes . . .'

Pachl/Schmidt: 'As I told you yesterday, if you phone, it's all high security there as well.'

Adler (cuts him short): 'Right!'

Adler still has doubts, but is reassured by Pachl/Schmidt's authoritative manner.

Adler: 'Mr Schmidt, from whom do I receive the contract? The written contract?

Pachl/Schmidt: 'There will be no written contract, do you follow me?'

Adler: 'Yes.'

Pachl/Schmidt: 'Now, listen. First of all, instead of eight we now only have six men. So out of 130,000 that only leaves 95,000. So let's . . .'

Adler: 'Hmm . . .'

Pachl/Schmidt: 'Yes, let's just say 110 . . .'

Adler: 'Hmm . . .'

Pachl/Schmidt: '. . . though that would, however, include the going home bonus or going home incentive.'

Adler: 'Of course.'

Pachl/Schmidt: 'We calculated that at about 5,000 marks per person. We have to assume that that's OK and that you'll pay out the money.'

Adler: 'That goes without saying!'

Pachl/Schmidt: 'And secondly, you must guarantee that they really are healthy, solid workers.'

Adler: 'They certainly are.'

Pachl/Schmidt: 'I mean it's not worth our while, if these people fall over after a couple of milliremes.'

Adler: 'No, no, they can take it, they'll stick at it.'

Pachl/Schmidt: 'And if you need some kind of ganger, that has to be a foreigner too.'

Adler (interrupts): 'Of course. But, Mr Schmidt, to get back to the point. Am I being commissioned by Würgassen nuclear power station?

Pachl/Schmidt: 'Yes.'

Adler: 'Is that it straight?'

Pachl/Schmidt: 'That's it straight. You know all there is to know. Why the reservations? Look, you ask me to let the cat out of the bag. I've come much more than half way towards meeting your request.'

Adler: 'Yes, that's true.'

Pachl/Schmidt: 'I don't know, for example, how much you're going to talk about this. On the other hand, if you do have any reservations, please tell me what they are, and then we can talk about it. But then you must . . .'

Adler (interrupts): 'Yes, of course I appreciate that, that everything has to be done with the utmost discretion, and that sometimes things have to be done incognito. I appreciate all that. Only, if someone comes to me and introduces himself: "My name is Schmidt, Würgassen nuclear power station," and I know that's not true . . . then I have, as I said, my doubts. What am I getting involved with? Am I really dealing with the power company or who am I dealing with? You know, I wouldn't like to be somehow acting in a criminally negligent way or laying myself open to criminal charges.' (Adler gives a slight cough.) 'Yes, Mr Schmidt, I would like to know whether my partner really is the power company?'

Pachl/Schmidt: '. . . Well, I'll ignore your remark about criminal negligence . . .'

Adler: 'Yes.'

Pachl/Schmidt: '. . . and possible criminal proceedings. If there's some problem on your side, you would have to let me know, of course.'

Adler: 'No, not on my side of things . . .'

Pachl/Schmidt (cuts him short): 'What might be involved?'

Adler: 'On my side, no problems at all. You'll get the people from me.'

A meeting place is fixed. Adler suggests the bus terminus in front of the central railway station.

Pachl/Schmidt: 'At two pm. We'll settle the financial and the transfer arrangements then as well. OK, Mr Adler, is that all right with you?'

Adler (well satisfied): 'Yes, of course.'

Suspicion has now been removed. The lust for profit makes Adler careless.

It's Thursday, 8 August, at 12 noon. Adler's temporary Turkish chauffeur has driven him to Duisburg-Bruckhausen in his 280 SE Mercedes to take delivery of the suicide squad. The car is not parked in Diesel Street itself, but round the corner, on the main through road, Kaiser Wilhelm Street, opposite the Thyssen coking plant. The luxury vehicle causes a stir in this slum street. Turkish women peep out anxiously from behind curtains, fearful perhaps that yet another demolition is being planned, or that for hygiene reasons, there are going to be compulsory evictions and the bricking up of dilapidated houses. Turkish children stand around the Mercedes at a respectful distance and pass their expert opinions on it. Adler doesn't quite know how to behave. He smokes one cigarette after another and constantly looks round. Sooty clouds pour out of the Thyssen chimneys, and a light wind blows the filth directly onto the nearby houses. One doesn't only smell the dirt, one tastes it, bites on the grains of soot, and sometimes the eyes smart. With certain sulphurous combinations – depending on the weather and the time of day – you feel yourself choking. The number of asthma and bronchitis victims in the district is above average. The children are extremely pale. I notice a small, slim boy of about five or six whose face looks as serious, tired, worn out and old as an adult's.

Although the sun was shining in Duisburg city centre, here it's a grey, dull day; here, the sun doesn't penetrate the factory clouds. I've been watching Adler from the other side of the street and sense how uncomfortable he feels here. For him, Diesel Street and its surroundings are the gates of hell. Hell, for him, lies inside the fences and walls guarded by the Thyssen company police. There, the air is even more unbearable and in addition there's the thunderous noise of production.

Adler has never come to our workplaces; that would weigh down his tender soul too much, and he would get nightmares. In his tailor-made suit Adler looks wholly out of place in these surroundings. He's almost as obscene and unreal as the spotless politicians on the election posters which in this district are not replaced by ads – except for cigarettes and beer.

Our 'final levy' consists of six Turkish friends who know the score. They are less surprised than I am by the nature and purpose of the job, and by Adler's brazen lack of conscience. This has been their experience and their reality for a long time. However, I haven't told them that I'm German, so as to avoid any distance developing between us. Adler might notice and become suspicious.

I guide our group to my flat in Diesel Street without Adler seeing us. Then I fetch Adler. He would prefer it if the 'people', as he calls them, came down to him on the street, but I say, 'Not good, too dangerous, because some no papers.' With this warning, I'm already engineering the intended end of the story.

'If I absolutely must,' says Adler, starting off for my flat. There's a strong smell of piss in the stairs. The toilets are all outside the flats. A drainpipe is blocked. Adler hastily stamps up the stairs beside me, and on the first floor I unlock the door and present my Turkish friends to him.

'Morning,' he says briefly, glances round the group, and counts them off, 'Two, four, six. Fine. Right, listen. Well – do you all speak German, anyway?'

'Yes, most can,' I lie. (I want him to make the effort of giving a little speech, to show himself up for what he is, even more.)

'We are a maintenance company in Oberhausen,' he introduces himself, 'and we've got the job of carrying out some repair work in Würgassen nuclear power station. It'll take two days and we need five or six people. We are being well paid for it, and you're going to be well paid too. So if there are still some

questions, just go ahead. I'll answer all your questions immediately.' He makes a frank and likeable impression. Someone
who's never had anything to do with him before could easily be
taken in by him. In order to draw him out even further, I have
arranged with my Turkish friends for them to put questions in
Turkish. I, with next to no knowledge of Turkish, translate
'freely', that is to say, I ask Adler those questions which seem to
me to be important. He hasn't noticed that I never talk to my
Turkish workmates in Turkish and that my German is by no
means the usual German that foreigners speak. By using
complicated figures of speech, it's sometimes possible for me to
elicit more differentiated statements from him. He doesn't
notice, since to him 'his foreigners' are nothing but beasts of
burden. As long as they labour and work for him without
complaint, he's the last person to harbour prejudices against
immigrants. On the contrary, he's one of the few who really
knows their value. It's only when they protest, and demand their
long overdue wages, that they become 'trash, rabble, robbers,
idlers'. 'Turkish colleague wants to know,' I ask him, 'how we
get there?'

Adler sells us the trip like a promotion man putting on a bus
trip with free coffee and cream cakes. 'Everything's free,' he
says, 'at three o'clock a bus will pick you up at Duisburg central
station, and a bus will bring you back again two days later. Digs
are free, meals are free, everything's free.'

'My friend here worry,' I tell Adler, 'perhaps tell him why 500
marks – so much money for so little work?'

Now Adler becomes expansive. 'Yes, now listen. The reason
is this. You know Germany. We have different kinds of power
stations. And we'll be working in a nuclear power station. It's
not producing any electricity at the moment, but is having a
general overhaul. And it's been discovered that there are *some*
things which have to be repaired. So that has to be done at very
short notice, because next week it must be supplying electricity

again. And it's also the case that, for example, nothing must get out to the papers about this little defect, because otherwise the "Greens" immediately get into the act, etcetera etcetera. And then they would have to shut the nuclear power station down, right.' And with undisguised loathing in his voice, 'You know, we have these little political groups in Germany . . . This job has to be done now, so that the power station can deliver electricity again next week. And they're going to pay *good money* for that, and you're going to get *good money too*.'

'Mr Adler,' I probe further, 'one say: always cheated by Germans.'

Adler swallows; to win time he pretends he hasn't heard, 'I beg your pardon?'

'He say, always cheated by Germans.'

'But have *you* ever been cheated by me?' counters Adler.

It's not the right moment to confront him with all his swindles, that he still owes me almost 2,000 marks, that he tried to trick me out of my wages altogether for some jobs, that he slipped part of the income tax and insurance contributions into his own pocket, 'etcetera etcetera'.

'Perhaps you say again yourself, how much you give to Turks,' I say, playing down the embarrassment of the situation. Adler makes himself comfortable, lets his new chauffeur give him a light, and settles down to present himself as a benefactor of the humiliated and oppressed. 'I have been working with Turkish employees ever since I set up in business on my own account. And up till now the Turkish employees have never let me down. It's always worked out well with them, in contrast to German workers, and I'm sure that I will continue working together with Turkish employees and giving them work.'

He calls it 'working together,' when he gets the money and lets others labour for him till they drop and die. And such 'social partnership' phrases like 'working with' and 'working together' are supposed to sound like music to the ears of those crushed by sweated labour.

'There are some threaten with deportation to Turkey,' I keep him to the subject.

'Yes, that need not necessarily happen,' he says generously. 'The reason we're not taking Germans for this job, I'll tell you this quite straight, is because they talk too much. They go away and talk. You, and I know that from our other Turkish employees, you keep your mouths shut. Do you follow me? That's why I'm not taking any Germans. You can forget about the Germans.'

'Ayth,' I point to a Turkish colleague, 'live in cellar . . .'

Adler cuts me short with a gesture. 'Good. Doesn't matter. I don't know anything.'

'Perhaps help sometime,' I press him.

And again, like most post-war businessmen, he polishes up his image. 'Help, of course. I'm always ready to do something for the poor. I grew up a Social Democrat, that is, I'm an SPD member. So I'm there to help the workers. So, for example we want to help these people, they'll be able to earn a few marks now, and if they have to go back to Turkey, you've got 500 marks or something . . . you've earned a few bob.'

I point to Sinan, another of the Turkish workers. 'He ask if work not dangerous?' His ensuing speech would have done credit to any spokesman for the nuclear industry. 'No, it's not dangerous. It's a large nuclear power station, and the safety measures are as rigorous as elsewhere in Germany. The German nuclear power stations are the safest nuclear power stations in the world. Thousands of people work on the site. There's no danger whatsoever.'

'Nothing ever happen?'

'In Germany there has never been an accident at a nuclear power station,' says Adler.

That may even be right as far as nuclear power stations themselves are concerned, although a jet fighter once crashed very close to the Würgassen nuclear power station. If it had crashed onto the plant, there would possibly have been a catastrophe of unimaginable magnitude. Nevertheless, people have often been injured in accidents in nuclear power stations, and the industry itself admits to five deaths.

For Adler, the work is 'not dangerous'. And not heavy either. And when I want to know, 'Must climb high?' he evades the question. 'Well, it's all inside the power station, I don't know, it's several stories high, isn't it?'

'He still want to know, what exactly job is?'

'It's repair work, machinery repairs, light repair work. But these repairs must be carried out. So five or six men are needed. We've worked it out, it can't be done any other way. We need five or six men to complete it within two days. The people will be sent in. The safeguards are there. You'll see that, with them, the human being comes first!'

That must sound a bit rich even to him, so he expands his statement: 'Nothing's allowed to happen to the people working there! The safety measures are very rigorous. Of course there's still a little radiation from a nuclear power station, even when it's not operating. But you'll be told how far you can go, and you'll be withdrawn immediately. A person's health is not put at risk. You'll see that for yourselves. I mean, otherwise you could tell them, we're going to stop work. You'll see that for yourselves. But there's one thing that's really important: we do the work, we get paid for the work and then we forget about it. Nobody says anything about a fault, for instance. The power station has made that quite clear. That's it, finished, over and done with. Till the next time. We often get jobs like this. We have to be very discreet, keep our mouths shut and work. Finish, over and done with. There's a lot of money in it. Right, that's everything sorted out. We leave at lunchtime today, the job is finished by Saturday afternoon at the latest, you'll be put down in Duisburg at the central railway station again, go home and the thing's forgotten. Get your money and nothing more's said. Is that reasonable?'

Awkward silence from my Turkish friends. Somewhere, the

fun has gone out of play-acting. Adler assures us of his reliability for the umpteenth time. 'All the men that I've employed get their money. There's no question about it, if we've come to an agreement. There will be 250 marks paid out tomorrow, 250 marks when the work's finished, all in cash. Ali here, my driver, will be there to look after you. Just listen to him, he'll also guarantee that you get your money.'

Yet again he emphasizes the perfection and social concern of the German nuclear industry. 'Work clothes will be provided there, work shoes will be provided. Helmets will be provided. Everything will be provided. But let me emphasize once more, you mustn't talk about it. Especially not with the newspapers . . .!'

With a grand gesture, he pulls a 50 mark note out of his briefcase, and hands it to me with the words, 'Right, you take the 50 marks so that the boys can get something to eat. They need to have some food inside them, a little something, so that they don't pass out as soon as they start work. Is that everything?' And as he's going out, he says patronizingly, 'All the best, boys. Till three o'clock. I'm sure I can rely on you. All right?' Fifty marks divided by seven. That makes 7.14 marks each for a last supper.

Two pm, Adler meets safety officer Schmidt and his assistant Hansen, in the Duisburg station restaurant. All the details are once again discussed quite openly and clearly, so that Adler can't talk his way out of it afterwards, by claiming he hasn't understood.

Herzog/Hansen: 'Mr Adler, we've received new measurements this morning. They exceed our worst fears. It will be a difficult, very tricky business. There's the radiation in the pipe which they have to get into . . .' (looks round the neighbouring tables, whispers) 'the radiation your people will get in one go is equivalent to 30 times the allowable annual dose. The results can be very serious.'

Adler: 'And what happens, for example, if it's not done?'

Herzog/Hansen: 'Then we can't rejoin the grid. Impossible! The loss of production would cost millions and millions.'

Adler: 'Yeah, it can't be helped. They've got to go in there and sort it out.' (And to reassure himself) 'Officially, I don't know anything. You need the people, I deliver, and they get on the bus. And you transport them to Würgassen. And basically I don't know any more about it. Finished, over and done with. I haven't done anything criminal. I can assure you that the men won't ask too many questions, they don't even know where Würgassen is . . . What does concern me is, how do I get my money? Does that go through the books of the power company?'

Pachl/Schmidt: 'It doesn't go through official channels, otherwise we wouldn't be acting in so discreet a way . . .'

Adler: 'With a deal like this, I naturally draw a few conclusions. I'm helping to pull you, let's say out of the shit. So you can also help me. I want the whole amount off the books.'

Pachl/Schmidt: 'It's a special category. It doesn't show up at all.'

Adler (greedy): 'Well, how are you paying? Cheque or cash?'

Pachl/Schmidt (remaining firm): 'First half cash, Second half crossed cheque.'

Adler: 'And the cheque will be from the power company?'

Pachl/Schmidt: 'Not directly. The cheque will be from a neutral source.'

Adler: 'I don't want the tax office to get wind of it afterwards!'

Herzog/Hansen: 'Have you had problems before?'

Adler: 'No, not if you meet your obligations. I always get my clearance certificates from the insurance scheme and from the tax office, and the employment office even sends me people, all above board.' (He laughs.) 'They don't want any problems. If they're paid fairly punctually they leave you in peace.'

Herzog/Hansen: 'What do you do if one of your people has an accident at work? Can you deal with it? I mean, we don't want them going to the doctor afterwards.'

Adler: 'That gets dealt with. My customer isn't inconvenienced at all. It doesn't show up in the accident statistics. We recently had an accident at Ruhr Chemicals. And the customer didn't have to worry about it. What's the worst that can happen? That they pass out on the spot?'

Herzog/Hansen: 'It could be tricky if someone keeled over when they were inside. He would be about 10 metres down the pipe.

Adler (unconcerned): 'Can't you pull them out with a rope or something?'

Herzog/Hansen: 'We'd have a try, but it's damned difficult. The pipe has a sharp bend. We have to make sure we don't use hefty workers who are big across the back.'

Adler (reassures him): 'Na, none of them are. They're all poor souls, who don't get enough to eat. They've got no meat on them.'

Herzog/Hansen: 'Well, we hope they're not going to drop right away. As far as the radiation goes, our experience is this: if there is serious contamination or incorporation, then the victims will have acute symptoms of radiation sickness within four weeks at the earliest – but by that time they must be out of the way. The symptoms would be hair loss, impotence, vomiting, diarrhoea, complete lethargy and so on. As far as long term effects are concerned – we've got no control over that anyway. If cancer occurs a year later, then by that time this job has been forgotten about.'

Adler: 'I mean, I'm not worried, I'm really not worried. I approach the whole thing very coolly. A job is a job and I realize that there are some things which happen in nuclear power stations which shouldn't become public.'

Herzog/Hansen: 'Well, just between the three of us, Würgassen is a scrapheap.'

Adler: 'Yes, I know, because of its age, for a start. Are you in fact the Mr Simon I once had dealings with a few years ago?'

Herzog/Hansen (oracle-like): 'Well, I'm not quite the person I appear to be!'

I come up to the table.

Adler: 'Ah, there he is. This is Mr Ali, who'll keep the gang together, look after them and keep an eye on everything.' (To me) 'Now, let me make this clear. What these gentlemen say, that's what you've got to do. Are the boys OK?'

Ali: 'They ask all the time, want to know everything, they are like children sometimes. Always ask, always ask. Some think will be like fight with dragon . . . will be so dangerous.'

Adler: 'Nonsense, nuclear power stations are safe, the safest in the world. I already told them that this morning. Safety measures, it's all there.'

'All understood,' I say. Adler sends me out to the 'troop' who have been waiting in front of the station all this time.

Once I'm gone, Adler says to the power station officials, 'He doesn't know what it's all about. They trust him. When he says something's going to be done, then it's done. He'll make sure that they don't do a lot of rubbish, that they do a proper job of work. They're like children, after all. If they ask questions, then they want proper answers.'

Herzog/Hansen wants to know if 'Ali' is 'a reliable man' too, and this yet again gives Adler the opportunity to play the role of benefactor and tell more of his lies.

'The poor bastard, I took him on about one and a half years ago. Do you know what he was doing to earn a living? Being a human guinea pig for some doctors. They were giving him injections.'

Herzog/Hansen: 'In Turkey?'

Adler: 'Here! In Germany! I can hardly believe that things like that go on. It's bad enough doing it to animals.'

Herzog/Hansen: 'That's what he was doing?'

Adler: 'That's what he was doing. He came to us, and I noticed him staggering around the place. So I followed it up, and asked him, what's the matter? Then he tells me, "I have got an injection again from doctor, I get 800 marks a week for it!" I said, "Now that's enough of that. That stinks. That's the end of that, son." He's a decent guy.'

Herzog/Hansen: 'What exactly have you told the people?'

Adler (reporting quite accurately): 'That they are going into the power station, that they have to do some urgent work which is necessary for the nuclear power station to rejoin the grid, that they've got to keep their mouths shut so that the press doesn't somehow catch on and that there's to be no fuss about it. I said, "The safeguards are there, German nuclear power stations are the safest there are. It that understood? You get protective clothing, you get everything, you'll be protected." '

Pachl/Schmidt: 'It's essential that they disappear within the next two weeks . . .'

Adler: 'They'll be gone within two weeks.'

Pachl/Schmidt: 'Gone with the wind.'

Adler: 'That's what's going to happen. Most important, I don't have a big office or anything, so no one else knows what's going on. I'm the only one who knows anything, and that's the way it should be done! You can rely on me. We'll manage everything!'

'We'll manage everything' is a guiding principle of Adler's and of most of the other suppliers of men to heavy industry and the building trade. 'We do everything' is the slogan of capitalism, or rather, one should add 'everything that makes a profit'. And if, until now (apart from experiments during the Third Reich when remains of concentration camp victims yielded fat and bones to the value of 11.50 marks per corpse), people are not melted down for soap, then that's not for reasons of humanity, but only because it's not worth making soap out of people.

Adler leaves the station restaurant with Schmidt and Hansen, to load the men onto the bus.

The problem was, we couldn't take the experiment as far as to hire a bus and drive it up to Würgassen. Adler would turn up there the next day, as promised, in order to collect half of his money. For a while I consider confronting him, quite concretely, with the murder that he assumes he's done. Eichmann, too, never actually saw the mounds of corpses; he was 'only' responsible for organizing the transport of those still living to the extermination camps. I had the idea of presenting Adler with the 'radiation injuries' of some Turkish friends in a little room of the 'Zur Kurve' Hotel in Würgassen, prepared by make-up artists: peeling facial skin, whole bunches of hair falling out, and lying in bed or on the floor in total lethargy.

Anyway, it's all plain enough. All that's missing is a conclusion that doesn't make Adler suspicious that something is being staged, causing him to flee abroad, wiping out clues and destroying incriminating documents. The best idea is for it simply to dissolve in front of his eyes, like an apparition. Like the genie of the bottle, which released, makes itself small again, returning to the bottle and – bang! Put the cork on!

When Adler, Hansen, Schmidt and I go up to the 'troop' to load them up, 'police officers' in plain clothes, flashing their cards, push their way between us. An ID check. Two of the Turks make a run for it, the others are 'marched away'. Everything happens very slowly as if it's a preliminary improvised rehearsal of a play. For Adler, it must be like a slow-motion nightmare.

There has almost been a serious mishap. One of the two friends, a headmaster and a Protestant minister, who were originally to play the plain clothes patrol (equipped in advance with handcuffs and toy revolvers) mistake Adler for Günter Zint, our undercover photographer; they go up to him and greet him. Pachl/Schmidt reacts immediately and makes the best of it. He introduces them, 'These are our security men from the power station, detailed here for this special job, they're keeping an eye on the square.' Adler is full of praise: 'Very well organized'. Only, how can we wind things up now? I discuss with my Turkish friends whether they can risk the intervention of a genuine police patrol. Some don't have their ID's with them, but it would make things all the more realistic if they were actually taken away to the police station.

One of us calls the police, giving an exact description of the place where a deal is being done with illegal Turkish immigrants. Five minutes later two police patrol cars with six officers drive up, they jump out of their vehicles and approach the group of Turkish friends. Then they see the photographer, Günter Zint, posted 15 metres further on, with his telephoto lens pointing at them. They correctly conclude that it's trained on them and suspect – as I later learn unofficially from the Duisburg CID – that a magazine wants to set a trap for them, to prove how easily and with what methods foreigners can be arrested, as the result of a mere denunciation. They return to their vehicles and clear off.

Now we're still no better off than before. Time is running out.

Adler is growing uneasy, because the 'power station bus' has still not appeared. Gesine, the girlfriend of Sinan in our group, saves the situation. From a student pub near the railway station, she fetches two customers, who can't, of course, be informed of all the details at such short notice. We only tell them that the simulated arrests are intended to help expose a big fish in the trade in illegal labour. They're prepared to help. One, it later turns out, is a town councillor of the Green Party.

The 'arrest' of our Turkish friends is correspondingly anti-authoritarian and friendly. Quite the opposite of realistic brutality. They virtually take our friends by the arm, when they 'lead them away'. However, as I said, Adler swallows it.

Ayth, who resists, has his arms twisted up his back. I run after them, and Adler, who still can't believe that the deal is falling apart in front of his eyes, calls me back, out of breath, to ask me anxiously, 'What's happening?'

'Police,' is all I say, 'arrest because no papers.' That was the magic word. His head drawn in a little, and at a noticeably swift pace, glancing in all directions, Adler hurries towards his Mercedes, which is parked beside a bus stop. He just about avoids running, presumably so as not to attract attention and because he owes it to his respectability.

He just leaves his business partners standing in the street. Pachl/Schmidt runs after him and demands an explanation. 'What's going on? Why are they all running away? How can this happen? You said there was no risk.' Adler, without interrupting his flight, and short of breath, says, 'Of course there's no risk. Just phone me up in the car.' And as he jumps into the Mercedes, which moves off right away, Pachl/Schmidt is still shouting after him, 'Mr Adler, we need you for this . . .'

Epilogue

So that everything ends properly, Pachl/Schmidt rings Adler up again, early in the evening. Adler on the phone is slightly embarrassed and tries to play things down. 'Yes, Mr Schmidt, that was a bit of a surprise this afternoon.'

Pachl/Schmidt (accusingly): 'Yes, what went wrong then, Mr Adler?'

Adler: 'I don't know either. The boys weren't quite clean. After all, I can't look inside their heads.'

Pachl/Schmidt: 'And how are we going to get out of this?'

Adler: 'It's all right, I've taken care of things, I've got some new people for you.'

Pachl/Schmidt: 'No, that's out of the question now, Mr Adler. You don't need to take care of anything any more, because we have now taken care of it ourselves. The problem had to be, as we told you, out of the way by 6 pm tomorrow. We thought you were a professional, Mr Adler.'

Adler (on the defensive): 'Well, two men out of the six . . .'

Pachl/Schmidt (interrupts him): 'Two men, two men, do you know what percentage that is, two men out of six?'

Adler: 'Yes.'

Pachl/Schmidt: 'You can work it out for yourself, Mr Adler, it's a third, Mr Adler, a third, 33.3 per cent, do you follow me?'

Adler: 'Yes, well, what are we going to do now?'

Pachl/Schmidt: 'Yes, what are we going to do now, Mr Adler? Everything was going like clockwork on our side, we had the two people keeping an eye on things, we had the bus – and you just drive off. And you're not even in a position to give us a coherent explanation. What's going to happen? We have to reorganize everything now – without you. Goodbye!' (He bangs down the telephone receiver.)

Half an hour later, I phone up Adler.

Adler immediately goes onto the offensive with me. 'What sort of people did you dredge up for me? They were nothing but criminals!'

Ali: 'But I say to you, two in cellar have no papers. Police took them.'

Adler (amused, laughs): 'Yes, I saw that.'

Ali: 'Others want money. Not their fault. Leave other work and now nothing.'

Adler (contemptuously): 'Now they're getting cheeky on top of everything else. Tell them the deal's dead. No money.'

Ali: 'But you say, you want to help them!'

Adler: 'Yeah, but they've got to work for it first.'

Ali: 'Police was at Diesel Street and want to know everything. I not there. Now I am to come and make statement . . .'

Adler (interrupts me): 'Yes, don't mention my name, of course! You mustn't, I can't have anything to do with it, right!'

Ali (innocently): 'What shall I tell them?'

Adler: 'Say, for instance, it was a Mr Müller or someone, who had promised some work, and you had spoken to the boys about it.'

Ali: 'If want to know, how he look like?'

Adler (pauses): 'Don't say anything – you don't know!'

Ali: 'Not know?'

Adler: 'And you don't understand anything. The best thing to say is that you don't understand any German.'

Ali: 'Yes. Can we not do something for friends?'

Adler: 'For the boys, no, but for you. We'll sort it out later. You should have seen my customer's face. There were really furious. What a mess! – Anyway, if someone asks, say a Mr Müller or somebody from Duisburg . . . you don't know where he lives, you don't know where his office is either. And you had organized it to get them a bit of work.'

Ali: 'Shall I say nothing about atom?'

Adler: 'Oh, no no no no, for God's sake!' (Laughing) 'Who did they catch, then?'

Ali: 'Two from cellar. They must leave now, go to Turkey.'

Adler (cheerful and, at the same time, relieved): 'Sent back to Turkey, poor guys! What a shame! But I would never have expected there would be so many policemen running around at the station!'

Ali: 'But it was you said, meet central station.'

Adler (reproachful): 'You should have said something to me beforehand, we could easily have done it somewhere else.'

The next day, Friday 9 August, Adler lets his new chauffeur, Abdullah, Ali's 'brother', pick him up at ten. He tours the banks within a considerable radius, good-humouredly notes the payments in his account book, picks up his share of the booty from the Remmert company, and during the drive chats to his new man, Abdullah, about his current worries.

Adler: 'Those are bloody long delivery times, you have to order a year in advance, to get the new model delivered on time.' (Growth at any price is still capitalism's motto, even if it's no longer expanding and exploding so violently. 'If there's no advance, then there's a retreat', is the fear of all generals, conquerors and capitalists right up to our own time. Given the economic situation, Adler is being modest.) 'I'm changing from the 280 SE to the 300 SE of the new series. That'll be in the autumn. This one will already be eighteen months old by then.' (His current model, with all the accessories and extras, cost about 100,000 marks, the new one will cost much more.)

Abdullah (changing the subject): 'Those two are sitting in jail now.'

Adler: 'They'll probably be deported. I feel really sorry for the boys. But on the other hand, let me say this. Probably it's actually better for them. What kind of life have they got here in Germany? They can't move about freely, can they?'

Abdullah: 'That's true really. In Turkey the sun's shining . . .'

Adler: 'Yeah, what are they going to do here? They live in a cellar here. Always frightened of the police. Don't have any work, don't have a home, they've got nothing.'

Abdullah: 'No work either.'

Adler: 'What keeps them here?'

Abdullah: 'Of course, Ali is a little bit sad now.

Adler: 'Well, yes. It just went down the hole. We shouldn't have met at the station. We should have met somewhere else. Shit! There are always police running around at the station.'

Abdullah: 'That was the trouble.'

Adler: 'Yeah, yeah.'

Abdullah: 'Do you think you'll get another contract from there?'

Adler: 'From them, sure. I've been in at Würgassen for a long time now, year in, year out, it'll keep going . . .'

Abdullah: 'They must pay very well too?'

Adler: 'Yes, we always get contracts from them. We never have any problems. At the moment, of course, he's in a foul temper. The worst thing about it is, with this customer, it's a really respectable shop. It's only very occasionally that one of their jobs isn't quite above board. They were frightened too because, for example, if that had got out into the paper or something, etcetera, etcetera, that the power station was faulty . . .'

Abdullah: 'They were even more worried.'

Both laugh.

Adler: 'They disappeared like a shot, ha ha. They were shitting themselves even more. Usually you only get into a nuclear power station if you've got a valid radiation pass. The German state lays that down. The management of the power station says, fuck that. The people get in anyway, without a radiation pass. That's already an offence! You've really got to watch it. They're breaking the German law and that's why they were frightened of the police.' (Laughs.)

Abdullah: 'But of course, they pay good money for that, no?'

Adler: 'They pay good money for that, because they're breaking the law. We're going against the law, you understand? And they pay for that. And that's a risk. If the German state knew what they were doing, even what they're doing now, then they're for it! Bloody hell! Every day's full of new surprises, isn't it?' (He laughs.)

Abdullah: 'When they took the guys away, I was pretty frightened.'

Adler: 'One of the policemen was holding two men at once, like this, right?' (He gestures) 'They might even have taken me as well. First of all, they would have asked dumb questions, and in my position I can't afford that. I don't want to have anything to do with the police.'

Abdullah: 'In Turkey, there aren't any laws like that.'

Adler: 'I know. It's much more free there. But here they make a law for every little piece of shit. Before you know where you are, you've broken another law. Here in Germany, you can really forget it. And then they're on top of you, and the sentences are really stiff. If that had got out, the manager of the power station would have gone to prison for at least a year. It's terrible. That's why you have to make sure that you don't get dragged into it. That you stay clean . . . Nothing could happen to me, anyway. If laws had been broken, it would have been by the people from the power station. They would have broken the law.

'They said to me, we need six men for some urgent repair work. I said, OK, you can have them. I don't know what you do with those six men. If you just let them in, like that, without a pass or anything, it's their problem, isn't it?'

Abdullah: 'I don't know anything about it.'

Adler: 'Forget it. We learn from experience. Next time, under no circumstances do we meet at the central station again. Yeah, that's for sure! Shit!'

This case was played through as a small-scale example of the worst possible type of case. Perhaps in reality, similar or worse contracts are already being carried out on a larger scale. If this investigation has contributed to alerting the sensitivity of the public and the media to these secret worlds, then our efforts have been worthwhile. Adler isn't the real target here. His criminal energy and imagination are not above average. Nothing would be more mistaken than to make a monster of him. He is one of many thousands who help to maintain and benefit from a system of boundless exploitation of, and disregard for, human beings.